The Perfect
CV

TOM JACKSON

The Perfect
CV

Stand out from the
competition and get the
job you really want

PIATKUS

Copyright © 1981, 1990, 1996, 2004 by Tom Jackson

This edition first published in the USA by
Broadway Books, a division of Random House, New York

First published in the UK in 1991
Reprinted 24 times

This edition first published in Great Britain in 2005 by
Piatkus Books Ltd
5 Windmill Street, London W1T 2JA
email: info@piatkus.co.uk

Reprinted 2005, 2006

The moral right of the author has been asserted

A catalogue record for this book is available from the British Library

ISBN 978 0 7499 2607 6

Text design by Mauna Eichner

This book has been printed on paper manufactured
with respect for the environment using wood from
managed sustainable resources

Data manipulation by Phoenix Photosetting, Chatham Kent

Printed and bound in Great Britain by
CPI Bath Ltd

Contents

PART ONE

Your Extraordinary Future

1

PART TWO

Your CV Workout

37

Acknowledgments

It is a big job to research and clarify the dynamics of a rapidly changing system as complex and multi-faceted as the employment market that impacts every employee, every employer, and every new job seeker out to connect with the economy.

To undertake this completely fresh look at the methodology of individual options and approaches for a CV-based career search took a lot of support from knowledgeable people.

Particular thanks to Marjorie Hendrickson – career consultant extraordinary – who could translate her face-to-face work with many hundreds of job seekers into powerful examples of the art of the CV as practised in real time with real people wanting real jobs.

Kris Garnier spent the better part of a year tracking down systems and protocols in every corner of the electronic job universe testing our assumptions and ideas and expanding our view of the way things were, how they worked, and for whom. Thanks, Kris.

James Grannel, a very smart computer science expert, helped us describe the methods for presentation to digital conversion, and tested a lot of our opinions online as a job candidate stand-in. He will never have a problem in his career given the quality of his work.

More than a dozen recruiters and career consultants added their ideas and experience and helped keep us on track with what was theory and what was practice. We acknowledge not only their insights but also their hearts, which are always driven by the human needs behind the job search.

Speaking of hearts; this book would not have been possible without the very hard, precise, passionate, focused, and inspired work of my wife and writing partner Elly Jackson, to whom my work is forever dedicated.

NOTE ON UK EDITION

Tom Jackson is well known for his innovative career development and job-finding ideas. His work is at the forefront of the movement for enhanced career freedom and mobility in the United States and in Europe, including the United Kingdom.

The CV techniques and examples in *The Perfect CV* have been proved to be dramatically successful throughout North America. Similar CVs are now being used successfully in the UK and other parts of Europe. They represent an enhanced way for you to take the initiative in your career search, to target the jobs you really want, and to gain the employer responses you need.

You will see that the CV samples in *The Perfect CV* are American (although terms that might be unfamiliar to UK readers and the text in general have been Anglicized). The CVs represent the best of Tom Jackson's trailblazing work in America. In presenting this material you are getting the best possible guide to constructing a hard-hitting tool for getting the job that you want. Use the information liberally, and make whatever adjustments and changes you feel appropriate.

Your Perfect CV

The Ultimate Job-search Tool

In today's digital job market, a perfect CV is more crucial than ever. It is the key to your career future. To think of a CV simply as a written account of your past employment is to ignore half the value and power of this critical data file. Formerly a one- or two-page printed document, the perfect CV today is the digital hub of your work experience, standard of living, and quality of life. It is the ultimate job-search tool: computer based, versatile, able to be launched in many forms – Internet, e-mail, and print. The process of creating the inventory and assembly of the information that will make it uniquely compelling is both more complex and more important than ever before. Don't believe that? Read on.

The foundations of the workplace are changing rapidly – not just in the digital world of CV exchange but more fundamentally in how employees are defined, what their options are, and how they need to present themselves. There is a trend towards over-specification and the specialization of jobs into ever-narrowing slots with rigid definitions. This reduction of work to cogs and slots reduces your options for deploying the full range of your skills and talents with versatility. Your perfect CV is designed to counter that.

Another workplace shift is the increasing demand by employers that employees surrender more of their personal values, family time, and security to a competitive business model based on shareholder value and short-term productivity drives. In addition, companies are increasingly outsourcing work to firms that offer employees less stability, reduced benefits, lower salaries, and fewer development opportunities. This throws out additional challenges for you to have your CV work harder to help you land the right jobs for you.

The Internet in corporate and employment service databases has become a central force in a revolution in the way people find opportunity. Information about possible job choices and selections is more available now than it ever has been. Whatever your goal is, you can blaze your own electronic path to it with a great CV. This book aims to provide all the information you need about how the job world has changed and how to take advantage of its new opportunities.

The multi-faceted CV is at the pivotal centre of your job search because it communicates your talent, employability, and lifestyle. We include *lifestyle* because if your personal qualities and desires are not factored into your job-targeting process, you might end up at the head of the line for a job you will hate. Your CV is the crucial and compact interface between who you are and what you can do and the practical economic world. Your CV stands for you in many ways.

Well-engineered CVs play a more important role in locating one-of-a-kind career and job opportunities than ever before. Focusing each CV to meet your own choices keeps you out of the mass-market job world and enables your self-definition in the market. The job-search process is much like good financial planning: you address key issues in your personal values *before* you put a budget together. In the same way, don't simply update your old CV; use the process to take a fresh look at yourself – your talents, needs, and values, and those of the market.

There are many useful books with good advice about the role of the CV, and lots of good material about typing and printing, and e-mailing and sending your well-shaped document by post. That information is included here too, to the degree it still applies. But this book adds more weight than others do to the thinking processes that go into uncovering, discovering, prioritizing, communicating, and delivering the priceless message that says, 'Here I am, look me over'.

The nature of your work – the jobs you hold – and the quality of your life are intimately connected. Joyless work casts a dark shadow on your 'time off'. The purpose of this book is to guide you in shaping your perfect CVs in a way that attracts the responses you want when you seek job opportunities that pay the bills and offer rich rewards beyond the salary. In preparing for this you will measure – perhaps more deeply than you ever have – your talent, passions, values, accomplishments, and experience and then translate these qualities into powerful and compelling language and form.

The Perfect CV is divided into six parts, each with a different approach to providing you the means to create a brilliant future for yourself. Each part is hands on and interactive. You are asked to first think about the new job-market challenges you face and then to take stock of which aspects of your future are most important to you. From there you define the formats that best meet your aims and learn how to communicate these aims to the right people. The last two parts show you how others have formulated their CVs to meet their own needs successfully.

I am dedicated to you as the author of your own success and self-expression. In this book I invite you to assert yourself against the conformity of conventional career thinking and job-search methods and build a launch pad for your independence and talent, one with enough power to take you right to the portals of real opportunities that dance to the same music as you do.

To make the most of what's best calls for you to dig deep into your true self – your core ideas and ideals. By dissolving old assumptions, beliefs, and job titles, and brushing off imagined limits, you are on an essential path to freedom from job worry.

Your CV will turn out to be an interactive database of talent and intention, working together like a great partnership with the purpose of presenting you to others in a way that gets them to want you on their team.

Good luck and work well for what you value.

Tom Jackson *Woodstock, NY*

The Parts

Starts by pointing your CV to an extraordinary future, one that reflects the best in you and your aspirations. Describes how recent shifts in hiring practices with emphasis on ever-narrowing job definitions and one-dimensional uses of electronic media could restrict your ability to get what you really want in your career future unless you take on some competitive and unconventional CV approaches. Shows what you need to reconsider and recalibrate to even get your CV read, and how to use the Internet to your advantage. Includes information about keywords, digital CVs, commercial job boards, and other rapidly changing methods.

Gives you a way to formulate what is most valuable and useful in marketing yourself. Includes assessments, worksheets, powerful words and phrases, and a process to identify the specifics needed to formulate your best CV. Doing this workout helps you define your job targets by inventorying your skills, capabilities, and accomplishments as well as your values, interests, and qualities. This database of information describes what makes you unique and competitively marketable. You can work in this section when and how you wish, return to it, revise it, and lift the information to use in CVs, covering letters, interviews, and more.

Details four different CV formats with examples. You learn when and how to use each of them and how to put together powerful covering letters and e-mails to strengthen and personalize your approach. Presentation (printed) and digital (electronic) formats are demonstrated and you learn how to make the conversion between them.

Describes unique methodologies for getting your CVs to the right people in the right companies in the industries you are attracted to: people who can make the hiring decisions. Shows customized covering letters, suggests e-mail strategies and follow-up approaches for gaining interviews.

Presents four in-depth situations where people faced specific challenges to their careers and worked them out by formulating special CVs, covering letters, and alternatives with a consultant. These stories show you how to get more mileage from your job search and create employment opportunities that go beyond conventional postings.

Provides forty selected sample CVs of different types and formats: presentation and digital forms; CVs with matching covering letters, before and after views, keyword summaries, and more. Each CV is notated by a CV consultant. The CVs and letters are those of Americans but the information they contain is universally applicable.

How to Make This Book Work for You

This book is designed to guide you in building sharp and hard-hitting CVs that will knock down barriers, unlock doors, and convey your strengths and values. It is an interactive book designed to turn information into ideas, ideas into actions, and actions into results. It will help you create CVs and covering letters that invite quality interviews with the employers you want to meet.

Read this book with a pencil or pen in hand. Answer the questions along the way. Circle things you agree with. Put question marks next to information you want to think more about. Underline things that are important to you. The CV Workout in Part Two can be done as you go along, or you can do it after you have studied the samples. There is no requirement to do any of the fill-ins along the way. Use only the material that helps you.

Throughout the book you will see sidebars and extra questions. Some ask you to make a quick note about yourself or jot down an idea, and others refer you to other pages for an example, a worksheet, or a way to dig deeper into a subject. Some of the exercises will uncover talents and values you may not yet be aware of. Take the time to go into these questions; what you discover about yourself will lead to a powerful and tangible pay-off not only in the CV documents, but also in what you discover by taking the time to do the work yourself.

The User's Guide

In the User's Guide are fifty-one frequently asked questions about using and preparing CVs. Each question refers you to places in the book where the answer is presented or an example is given.

Partnering

Find a person – a friend or a professional – who can help you in this work. This should be someone committed to helping you make the best possible case for your capability and talent. Have this person help you highlight your skills, identify good job targets, discuss the formats and covering letters you will use, and edit your writing. If necessary, use a second friend with strong language skills who can double-check your writing.

The Perfect CV User's Guide

ANSWERS TO THE TOP 51 CV QUESTIONS

Questions	Page Numbers
1. Why do I need a book to help me write a good CV?	3, 10
2. Wouldn't it be smarter to get a professional to write my CV for me?	6
3. I already have a CV – should I update it or start fresh?	7
4. How do I use my CV on Internet job boards?	15, 16, 95
5. I don't have any real experience. How do I write a CV?	28
6. I sent my CV to an electronic distribution service six months ago, with no response so far. What do I do next?	24
7. I've heard that employers prefer the chronological format to all others. True?	67
8. Why do I need a printed CV when many job transactions are now digital?	65, 96
9. Is there a limit to the number of pages I should use?	66
10. I'm responding to an online job posting. How do I send a CV?	97, 106
11. What do I do if I've been out of work for a long time?	78, 87
12. I know the company I want to work for, but I don't know if they have any openings. What kind of CV do I use?	111, 114
13. How do I e-mail a CV?	103, 106
14. Is a covering letter just a formality or will someone read it?	121, 124
15. Should I use an objective statement?	89, 92
16. What is an ASCII CV?	99
17. How do I write a good CV if my past work is completely different from what I am looking for?	74, 78
18. Should I include my current salary on my CV?	84
19. I don't know the field I want to be in. How do I write a good CV?	68
20. I want to start my own business. How do I prepare a CV?	28
21. I didn't go to college, but I worked my way up to a well-paid managerial job. Do I include this?	68, 69, 78
22. How do I put together a CV when all my experience has been with only one company and they are now out of business?	86
23. I have been in my own business for twelve years now and want to go and work for someone; what kind of CV do I use?	70, 74
24. I have been looking after my children for twelve years, during which time I have not been in paid employment. How do I account for that on my CV?	78, 189
25. What are keywords and how do I use them?	31, 32
26. Nothing's perfect. What is a 'perfect' CV?	6, 10, 11
27. How many years of my career should I describe?	68
28. What is a scannable CV?	98
29. Do employers list all job openings on their websites?	23, 113
30. How much detail do I give about my personal life: family, children?	83
31. I have several good references. Do I include them with my CV?	83

PART ONE

Your Extraordinary Future

The material in this part is dedicated to your having an extraordinary future, and to enhancing the role your CV will play in making that happen for you. Since changes in the working world have made that ever more difficult to achieve, knowing how the rules have changed, and how to deal with these changes, has become essential.

In the past half dozen years, the work world and job market have altered substantially, reducing the range of opportunities available to a person and narrowing the employment process in a way that cuts back individual choices. Traditional job-search methods – person to person, face to face, looking beyond the immediate job to a longer-term career relationship, and honouring the match between the inherent values of the person and the company – have been devalued. New productivity-driven hiring and outsourcing practices have largely replaced them. Corporate productivity priorities – shortsighted in my view – have pigeonholed talent; the Internet has made it easy to fill slots and almost impossible to discern qualitative and subjective criteria. Despite this stifling environment, countercurrents are available that allow you to take charge of your future if you are willing to act strategically and independently. This book shows you how.

The better you understand today's rules, and how to break them when necessary – with your own agenda in the forefront – the more successful your job campaign will be. In this part you will learn how market forces impact your CV preparation, design, distribution, and success. Work on your CV itself begins in Part Two.

Contents of Part One

Point Your CV to an Extraordinary Future

Who Are You, and What Are You Going to Do About It?

The perfect CV process starts with knowing who you are and where you want to go in your life (your job targets). Right up front you need to know how important it is to target the kinds of work that will make the most of your best. Without job targets it is hard to focus your CV. You are invited to merge your goals for your standard of living with the quality of your life. Not to focus on both will shortchange you: if you accept work you don't value personally, you will not perform at your best. If you try to squeeze the quality of your life into just after-hours and weekends, you will limit yourself.CV preparation is not step one

James F.: I spent six years as a title insurance researcher. I had a good salary, and I was given more responsibility in the work I did with the law firm that used our services. When the two companies merged, I became 'redundant', as they put it. I sat down and listed my work and was about to send out this chronicle of deeds and releases and eleventh-hour deals I helped facilitate, when I had lunch with a mortgage broker I often met at the closings. She said the mortgage refinance work she and her company were getting was booming with the low interest rates, and they were making lots of money brokering these deals. I actually already knew this, but she got me thinking. If she could do it, why couldn't I?

I asked her for a copy of her CV to review for my own future. Then I saw that I knew how to do almost everything she did, and I was sure I could do the same work myself. I appointed her my career consultant, and she pointed me to the additional information I needed to learn – not much – and the credentials I needed to have (few). I spent a weekend redoing my CV from chronological to functional format, and targeted my next job as a mortgage broker. She introduced me to a few people, and I looked in the area Yellow Pages for mortgage brokers, talked to a few mortgage brokers, and asked if they would be my references. No problem. I had half a dozen interviews and two offers. One was to be an assistant managing closings until I got all my credentials locked down and learned the ropes – and that was it. I was a mortgage broker. Not such a big deal, I know, but more flexibility, more responsibility, and, with some commissions, a 40 per cent increase in compensation. My first CV – and the way I thought about myself – wouldn't have done it. Believe me, the time was worth it, and I now know that my next change will be even bigger.

In the conventional employment process, a CV is ordinarily limited to snapshots of the past: what you have done, your education, past employers, a few keyworded skills, and your job titles. Commercial CV services follow this simplistic standardized approach. It saves time for them and makes preparation easier from a distance; it also turns you into a homogenized product, easily distributed to digital machinery heavily oriented towards simple yes–no answers. By listing only past job functions, duties, and titles, CVs can make a work history too narrow or job-specific and limit your opportunities for future change, development, and flexibility.

In the perfect CV process, you win in many ways: not only do you end up with a more powerful CV, but also your thinking is opened up about both your present and future strategies. You become more comfortable and conversant with your talents and motives. The more you learn about yourself, the stronger you become. We strongly recommend that rather than update an old CV, you start the process all over from the beginning. This will give you a fresh look at your future.

Targeting your CV to specific opportunities takes more time than simply applying to whatever jobs are on someone's laundry list. The CV that is targeted in advance has more power than one that simply follows a skills template or is a standard conventional listing of where you've been and what you have done. You need to go beyond what's conventional.

Conventional Knowing the basic kind of work you want to do, you send your standard chronological CV to appropriate jobs where you see them. For example, say you are good in sales, have had several sales jobs, and have prepared a chronological CV listing three sales positions. You find four sales openings online: car sales at a local dealership, heavy-equipment sales for a plant in a nearby town, a job selling kitchen installations at a major store, and a position as a corporate sales trainer. You send off your standard sales CV. Perhaps you get a form response or two, perhaps you get an interview and an offer.

Unconventional You go through the CV Workout in Part Two and in doing the exercises discover that your characteristics and interests suit you particularly well for a sales job as a yacht broker. You do the research, talk to a couple of people in the field, figure out which aspects of your past success and demonstrated capabilities most apply, and rewrite your CV to reflect those. By going online and reading *Yachting Monthly*, you identify twenty yacht brokers in the area where you want to work and send your newly customized CV to them. You get five interviews, and confirm for yourself that you're heading in a direction you like, working with the types of customer you are comfortable with in a location you want. You also now have several new contacts to talk to about your strategy.

Job targeting means rethinking what you're doing and asking how satisfying it will be in the next few years. Even if you are staying in the same general field, aim for the types of work you can prosper in, and emphasize the qualities and skills that fit those. This gives you a competitive advantage, because unfocused CVs are the biggest glut on the market. It also gives you a quality-of-life advantage when you're hired.

At a higher level, job targeting reflects your personal vision of the future. It is a way to look further than you ordinarily do towards what is really possible for you. It is an exercise of imagination about your future, and it need not be constrained by self-imposed limitations.

Can you imagine a future that is close to ideal for you? Can you start to incorporate that into your job targeting? Try it.

Participate:

Here is a quick warm-up for the CV Workout in Part Two.

A job I am now exploring is:

_____

_____

_____

The skills I need to demonstrate to be successful in this job are:

_____

_____

_____

The types of industry information (companies, products, trends, names) I can use to help build my contacts include:

_____

_____

_____

One crucial piece of information I need to know before getting my CV out to the right people is:

_____

_____

Another Warm-up:

Today I am a:

_____

_____

_____

If I looked at myself through a different set of lenses, I could be a:

_____

_____

_____

or a:

_____

_____

_____

2

The New Rules

A perfect CV is a full-strength partner in finding the kind of work you seek, whether it be in landing a competitive summer job, making the transition from school to work, changing careers, starting your own business, or being a consultant. It is not just a page or two that lists words and phrases in a logical order and is sent to employers. That is a regular CV. The CVs and covering letters you produce with this book will go beyond the traditional and commonplace. They will be a powerful and unique expression of who you are when you are at your best. You will learn how to get that information into the hands of those who can put you to work at what *you* want to do.

It is likely that since you last produced a CV from scratch, three major influences have changed the job-search and CV rules. These are:

- The Digital Job Jungle: thousands of commercial and employer-driven Internet job-search engines and services evolved during the dot-com boom, elevating the role of job-search technology in the process.

- The growing tendency of companies to very narrowly define and describe their work opportunities to match their internal (and ever more structured) processes and procedures. We call this the Cog Syndrome: matching people to the needs of the machine, instead of designing the machine's capabilities to enhance people's skills.

- A growing desire among employees for jobs that meet personal as well as financial goals. As salaries are devalued, benefits constrained, workloads increased, and family time increasingly intruded upon, employees are taking the initiative to define exactly what job opportunities satisfy their unique values and needs.

Today's Perfect CV

A perfect CV arranges your skills, capabilities, accomplishments, education, and values in a document that presents you as the perfect person for the job.

Like a perfect tennis serve, a perfect golf swing, or a perfect omelette, a perfect CV takes more effort than simply copying what others do. Doing the extra legwork pays big dividends. Your rewards come as much from the process of thinking and defining what you want and what you have to offer as from the finished CV.

Ask yourself why there are thousands of electronic and personal services, dozens of copycat catalogues and templates, and numerous books to help you tell a prospective employer what you can do that makes you valuable to their organization.

Here's why – most people have an internal resistance to expressing really good things about themselves. They often have difficulty taking risks in their careers, being creatively assertive, and going beyond the obvious employment processes to find something special. Out of 150 students at a lecture I gave, 125 had done nothing to further their job searches outside the standard college recruiting services – and this was at a time when employment of new graduates was at its lowest ebb in years. Often, people are afraid that if they go after something terrific, they will be disappointed or rejected. Listen to what some knowledge-able employment counsellors have said:

Chris J.: *I have seen numerous top students – many with high qualifications under their belts – quail at the thought of sitting down in front of a blank sheet of paper and listing what they do best. I am concerned about how they will get through an interview.*

Jennifer B.: *People with successful job histories often show up with an old CV and want help in updating it. When I ask if they want to continue in the same career direction for their next job, the looks on their faces say something like, 'Well, don't I have to?' In discussion I find they hadn't even thought about changing direction, even if the work they have been doing is completely uninspiring for them.*

Bob B.: *I'm surprised at how a really talented employee can tell you what his duties have been in past jobs, but has trouble telling you what he actually accomplished. Is it shyness?*

Rebecca T.: *Lots of people are willing to pay a substantial amount to an unknown firm, with whom they have little contact, to do a standardized CV for them. It's like paying someone to go to the gym for you. What would they say if an interviewer asked, 'Who wrote this CV for you?' What does it say about their ability to do the job?*

TODAY'S CV RULES
(Circle the number of each item particularly relevant to you.)

1. Using technology is preferable to having it use you. A digital CV is the main contact medium for many employers. Not crafting your CV consistent with Internet and search technology will severely limit your reach.

2. Prepare CVs in both presentation (designed for printed copies) and digital (electronic delivery) forms. Understand the implications, limitations, and strengths of each.

3. Take the time to do it right. There are very few jobs that do not require a CV as a prerequisite to even being considered as a candidate.

If you are experienced in a computer graphics, design, or IT field you should consider (if you can do it well yourself) creating an *online portfolio* that is a website and not only has internal links to your CV but also separate categories for:

Accomplishments	Education
Work history	References
Computer programs and equipment worked on	E-mail contact for messages
Sample design gallery	

Electronic portfolios show you are computer literate and can help set you apart. Unfortunately, since not every employer will take the time to look at them, for the moment you should also follow the other suggestions described in this book. Use of online portfolios will grow over the next few years as job market pressures ease up.

4. The quality of the opportunities you are considered for is a function of the quality of your CV and how you get it delivered.

5. Know yourself and what you want. Until you have examined and weighed both internal factors (your values, interests, skills, accomplishments, capabilities) and external factors (growth companies, corporate values, niche opportunities), you are not equipped to make a compelling case for the kind of work you seek.

6. Gear your CV towards where you want to be by focusing on your future career or job goals. If you rely only on past jobs, you will be preparing a historical document that tells where you have been, not where you are headed.

7. Customize your CVs for the individual jobs you are after. One size does not fit all. You are an individual with distinction; show it.

8. Target delivery of your CV precisely. The best CV in the world will not help you unless it gets to the right person.

9. Avoid generalities. Use objective and summary statements that are custom tailored to each separate job target. An objective statement tells the reader what you want, and a summary statement shows why you should be considered for the job.

10. Pay close attention to keywords and skills descriptions so you will pass unimpeded through screening filters (this is explained on page 33). At the same time, include material that demonstrates success and accomplishment related to the specific job so the human reader is motivated to see you.

A good CV can make you more likely to:

- Discover the best career directions to target for your future

- Get interviews with employers you want to meet

- Feel comfortable speaking about your accomplishments

- Make more money by stressing your ability to add value

- Adapt your skills to several kinds of work

- Take risks in your career development

3

Master the Digital Monster

The Internet is the most significant force to enter the job-search and employment process in ten years. Its attraction is in the speed with which it can locate simple job listings. Its shortcoming is that, being public, it invites commercial services that promise more than they can deliver. Many skilled people are distracted by the commercial hype from taking the time to use the Internet's broader resources to discover what will really serve them in their future careers.

In addition to the high-profile websites that advertise extensively and compete aggressively for market share, such as Monster, there are hundreds of industry-specific job boards that represent trade groups, professions, and journals. There are community sites, headhunter sites, and publishing and newspaper sites. There is also a large number of company job sites that tell you all about the organization, its products, and current opportunities. For a list of many different job-search sites, just go to your favourite search engine and type in the words *job boards* or *job listing services*. You will have hundreds to choose from.

Is this a good thing? Yes. Is it a bad thing? Yes. Your success depends on what you want from the digital medium, and how you use it. According to a recent study by the international outplacement firm

DBM, fewer than 10 per cent of its successful job finders got their positions from commercial Internet job services, and 35 per cent got connected through personal networks and referrals. The balance got placed through personal effort (using the Internet their own way, for example) and through private recruiters, newspapers, and state employment services.

There are some important things to consider about commercial job sites. First, watch out for the hype. Don't believe there are millions of jobs and recruiters watching and waiting for your superb qualifications to show up on the site.

SHORTCOMINGS OF ONLINE JOB-SEARCH SERVICES INCLUDE:

- Commercial sites usually charge employers to list jobs, so they will pick and choose which ones to use, which means you will have to register with numerous sites. Many other employers do not want or need to pay to list jobs. Reaching the full market of prospective openings online is impossible, yet you might be deluded into thinking you have broader exposure than you really do.

- Search terms are shallow. They tend to be simple job-function listings, making it harder for you to find a broader match.

- Posting your CV to the CV banks associated with these sites is often done through simplistic 'fill in the blanks' profiles. When you cut and paste your own CV it will be converted into ASCII text and most formatting will be lost, so it is likely to look unpolished to prospective employers. (See page 99 for more information on formatting ASCII.)

- CV banks claim to store data on millions of job seekers. You will be just one of these. Don't stop your regular job-search activities as you wait for your CV to be found in this electronic haystack.

Job-listing sites face declining revenues as fewer employers pay to post listings, so to supplement revenues many sites are now offering a 'premium service'. This means that if you pay, your CV will pop up at the top of the search list when an employer looks for certain keywords. Some sites will give you a higher ranking for more money.

Cog Syndrome

Cog Syndrome refers to the growing corporate practice of introducing ever-narrowing definitions for work positions using keywords, phrases, functional titles, and skill lists as filters in the screening and hiring process. As more business processes get automated and people get hired to fit into these processes, the industries look for ways to find just those skills needed for that narrow work. This dices each job into small functional equivalents and leaves out how and where the person can grow or contribute in other areas in the future. When that process is replaced or outsourced, so, too, are the people working within it.

Digital job searches are very basic. To post a CV you register, fill out a profile form asking you to list a number of 'keywords' – simple skill or job-function language – and a brief set of data about yourself. You may post an existing CV by cutting and pasting it into their input screen. Sometimes there are boxes you can tick, and of course the basic contact information. Once your CV is entered, the key terms and phrases are analysed, and those that meet basic criteria are indexed and/or compared against a set of search terms that employers have entered and tied to their needs. These terms are mostly functional skills lists, company names, degrees, and job titles. One of the problems with the entry and search process is that there is no predetermined vocabulary, so if you have terms on your CV that are slightly different from the employer's, yet mean the same thing, you might be missed; or if you have a phrase that is unique and would make sense to a human, the computer might not pick it up. Another limitation is that there is little or no way to use qualitative terms (fast, accurate, creative, successful) or to define accomplishments you have achieved.

This strict classification by keywords is the way general employment works for the biggest firms. Mass-market jobs on the Internet tend to be of a kind that lend themselves to this kind of codification. Unfortunately, the narrower the scope, the less opportunity to be versatile, creative, and independent. Many employees and job seekers tolerate this conformity since having any job is often better than making waves and losing what they have, or not getting hired.

On the other hand employers also want and need a range of employees who have the qualities of versatility, imagination, intuition, and leadership – the kinds of things that are not measurable in the rigid terms of Internet hiring protocols. These employers tend to be people who use specialized recruiters, do internal networking, or find their way around the system. This is where having the right CV pays off in a big way.

The more you understand about how the market works, the better able you are to stay outside the mechanized system and create your own job relationships with CVs that offer more than keywords and phrases.

In the US, a recent story from the *New York Times* tells of a woman whose CV came up first in a list of 2,348 search results for a systems administrator in the New York area. She said she had paid $40 (about £20) for a listing upgrade because she had been getting no responses from employers. 'The number of searches that it's come up in has doubled since I did it,' said the woman, but here's the catch: Although her CV received more exposure, it did not lead to a single phone call from an employer. 'It hasn't worked one way or the other yet,' she said. 'I'm not really sure if it was the right thing to do or not.'

There are also collectors, or aggregators, who promise to pack up your digital CV and supply it – along with hundreds of others – to a full list of search engine connections and recruiters, who will then multiply it even further. Many of these are triple-marketed to other job banks that also want to be able to boast about the sizes of their databases. You might be listed in several systems you didn't even know existed.

With all these opportunities, the odds appear to be in your favour. Are they, though? Not necessarily. It could very well turn out that simply sending your CV out like spam into the digital job jungle will put your complete identity, history, and earning power in hundreds of different locations for a dozen different purposes, and you'll never be able to retrieve it.

Here are two excerpts from a frequent web and e-mail advertiser in the US to make my point. First, the lead-in was made to look like a newspaper quote:

LOS ANGELES – January 13, 2003 – So, you're considering putting your CV on Monster, HotJobs, CareerBuilder, Dice.com, and a ton of others. But you're wondering, is it worth the time?

The answer is yes. Read on . . .

There still are millions of jobs listed among all the top career sites. With companies currently staffing for their 2003 business plans, this is the BEST time to put your CV on ALL major career sites. Additionally the top 50 career sites are reported to be searched by 1.5 million employers and recruiters daily!

This was followed by a pitch to use this company's CV-aggregation service to forward your CV to *all* of these sites plus hundreds more . . . 'and the list is growing daily'. Sounds great. But when you go online and look closely at the fine print of this firm's privacy agreement, here, among other things, is what you will find:

You are responsible for maintaining the confidentiality of your information, user name, and password. You shall be responsible for all uses of your registration, whether or not authorized by you.

You hereby further convey to [name of company] power of attorney to sign on your behalf (whether on paper or digitally) specifically indicating to each of these third party career websites that you have read, understood, and agree to abide by *their* terms [emphasis added], conditions, rules, and regulations.

By entering into this Agreement you're accepting full and total responsibility for the actions [name of company] performs on your behalf and at your request, as if you had performed those actions yourself.

By submitting your Personal Information to the Site you automatically grant [company] the royalty-free, perpetual, *irrevocable* [emphasis added], non-exclusive, transferable right and license to use, reproduce, modify, adapt, publish, distribute, translate, create derivative works from, perform and display such Personal Information (in whole or part) worldwide or to incorporate it in other works in any form, media, or technology now known or later developed, without restriction or compensation. In addition, you warrant that all so-called 'moral rights' in the Personal Information have been waived.

Did you know this is what you were agreeing to? Protect against identity theft by knowing exactly whom you are sending your CV to and what their privacy policies and practices are. Make security a priority. If you are using commercial CV distribution services consider using a post office box in place of your home address. Use e-mail but no phone number. Include this statement: *To protect identity certain information has been left off. Complete information will be provided to interested parties in response to e-mail.* Some candidates will leave off the name of their current employer, using a statement like: *major financial market leader.* Given the pitfalls, let's look at how you can get the most out of the digital job universe – which, although no panacea, is still the most amazing set of resources for job seekers ever created. To get the most from these resources – particularly in a tight job market – be prepared to put at least as much time and effort into preparing and marketing your perfect CV as you would into an essay at college.

I sent out CVs for eighteen months and didn't get one response. . . . Finally I just went into a high-priced local restaurant and asked to see the chef, told him how skilled I was as a home cook, and convinced him to give me a try in his kitchen. I became full time in a week. It pays less than I'm used to, but I love the work.

Laid-off airline worker

CV broadcasting used to be done by post and now is done on the Net – but it has never been very successful. To spend eighteen months sending out CVs is a waste of time. Like playing the lottery, it is tempting because there is always possibility right around the corner, but at its root, it is backward. The forward way is to contact selected people first, discuss the position, and then send a CV. This takes effort, however, and many people are not willing to take it on until they have run out of their redundancy pay.

Think of how the former airline employee got the job she has: she beefed up her courage and sense of capability, knocked on the door, and got a trial job that became permanent. She could have done that fifty times in the first six months, and not just at a random local restaurant. She could have created a set of opportunities to choose from. Lesson: don't broadcast.

The Hidden Job Market

The hiring process has been so automated and digitized that it takes guerrilla tactics to make it work to your advantage. This includes knowing how to target your CV, having the right buzzwords to get through the various search filters, finding the right people to get it to, and, perhaps most important of all, identifying work opportunities that fit your targets before they get advertised publicly – while they are still part of the hidden job market.

Listen to Philly Jones, placement agent:

> I love the recruiting business – making money by knowing about people, using good social skills and just enough plain common sense to stay ahead of the robotic competition. The process is very simple: we get electronic job-opening listings from companies and the various recruiter networks we know about. Then we find CVs, either electronically or by more

Common-sense Basics

Even though there are many strategies and tactics, formats, fill-ins, and do's and don'ts in this book, what I am recommending here is not so far from applied common sense. Consider how you usually use the Internet. You decide on the information you want, the facts you need, the ideas you want to explore, the products you want to research or purchase, the things you want to learn, the people you want to connect with, the addresses you need, the schedules, definitions, news events, and other content – mostly public – that you want to survey or review. You turn to your favourite websites for those things that you are already familiar with, or to one of the wizard-like search engines that give you 50 to 200,000 places to look in under one second. You are in the driver's seat all the way and can elect to connect to or skip over whatever is served up to you. You will do the same with a great CV approach.

Next, consider how you think about your work life. You have strengths that you know about, skills you have learned, accomplishments you're proud of, jobs you've held, functions you've performed, functions you've not yet performed but probably could, preferences as to work style, time and income trade-offs, quality of life considerations, family needs, learning and personal development goals, and personal values that are important to you. Lots of variables form the backbone of your life. Common sense would have you factor all of these into your job choices if you can.

You also have your own current situation: happily employed and looking to plan your future, bored with your current position and wanting to improve on it, worried about being laid off and preparing yourself for that eventuality, committed to changing your career direction, looking at a change in family requirements – like children – and how to adjust to these new circumstances, out of work and considering this as an opportunity to reinvent your future, just laid off and working with an outplacement or career coaching firm, or out of work, feeling broke, and worried about your survival. Each situation is different, and each has its emotional and motivational components. It is important to make sure that your career campaign includes all relevant considerations.

traditional methods. We match the two in an artful way, and then get the company and candidate to fall in love. Yes, it's that simple. But pay attention to the word *artful* and the words *common sense*. Our competition is the commercial placement services, and as automated as they are, they come up short in both elements: common sense and artfulness.

What we do that makes us special is simple, and I'll probably regret publicizing it. When we get a job posting, we assume it is probably a standard form pulled up by someone who isn't even near the business end of the company, or a repeat of the same position last time they had an opening in that skill set. So before we take it in, we get ourselves on the web, look up the firm on Google, find out about their earnings, the latest news in the field, changes in management. We talk – not e-mail – to a few people we know in the company or at a competitor and take the pulse of what is on people's minds at the firm TODAY – like the big oil-rig contract in Iraq. Once I know what to look for, I turn to the candidate side with all that in mind and find people with, say, Middle Eastern experience or something else that relates to the job type I'm filling. By knowing what's really going on, I can slant my search for candidates. Commercial placement services' computerized systems can't do that. Like with everything else, if you go a bit further than the system, you're ahead of the game. Is that rocket science? I call it common sense.

If you are serious about a perfect CV leading to the job of your dreams, you will want to put an important principle into play. Simply stated: *80 per cent of the available jobs on any given day are not advertised or published.* This pool of unadvertised opportunity is called *the hidden job market.*

Here's a corollary: *through imaginative use of the Internet – **outside the 'official' job-search sites** – you can find out almost anything you want about companies that are hiring.* And since the more you know in advance, the better your chances of putting the right CV in front of the right person, this research is part of your perfect CV preparation process.

We are making an important distinction here. The Internet has two faces: a commercial fast-buck side and a source-of-real-information side. If you want to take hold of your future, you must know how both sides work. Get all the information you can from all sources, and use it intelligently to put together a custom-tailored CV and delivery process that go beyond the commonplace.

The hidden job market is based on this reality: in any company, staffing is not even and predictable. New projects, new problems, new products, competition, retirements, and people leaving all cause continual changes in roles, people, numbers, and budgets. Even when a company is laying off people with certain skills, it often hires others to get different jobs done. New opportunities aren't rushed to the job-posting services or human resources. There is an informal process – sometimes taking months – in which a new need is anticipated, a retirement is planned, a new product is in the wings, a new contract is in the works. Internal placement is considered, people are asked for referrals, and nothing is announced publicly. The right unsolicited CV, read by someone who knows that it is relevant to a new position in the making, is a real contender. Most employers would rather hire out of a small group of possibilities than put a new job prospect out on the network, where hundreds of thousands will hear about it.

Given that in average times turnover in jobs is around 20 per cent per year, you can calculate easily that for every thousand jobs in the market, there are at least two hundred openings per year. This doesn't include new jobs: the labour force has been growing for the last twenty years. Since the time during which a job moves from anticipated opening to external announcement could be three to ten weeks, you can see that there is a big window you can crawl through. What it boils down to is this: in the unadvertised hidden market for talent, six out of ten companies will have nothing at the moment, two will have something cooking that is being circulated internally, and two will be within a few weeks of an official opening. It is these last four companies that you want to find.

Why is this important to you in writing your CV? By knowing there is constant change, you can make your career campaign an ongoing process, keeping your attention on what is happening in a variety of places and directing highly customized CVs to the right place at the right time.

Moreover the tools for probing the hidden job market are the very Internet-based research tools promoted here. Spending two hours learning how to master the search engines could easily double your job-search effectiveness.

Making the Monster Work for You

To make the most of the Internet, step away from the shortcuts and take an unconventional approach. Don't file your CV into a passive database or CV broadcasting service and sit around waiting for news.

Reverse the logic and use the public job-search services as a way of identifying the kind of job situations you are looking for. When you locate what meets your criteria, do not simply fill out an application template or send a digital CV. Instead, construct a strategy that will get you face to face with a real person who can make the hiring decision or influence it.

Here is the proven five-step approach recommended for harnessing the digital monster in creating your own job opportunities. This is expanded upon in Chapter 10.

SEARCH FIRST, SEND CV LATER – BY THE NUMBERS:

1. **Start with specific job targets in mind.** It makes little sense to reach into the vast dimensions of the job market without a target of some specificity.

2. **Identify specific locations where you desire to live and work.** To embark upon a national search when you really wouldn't consider moving out of London is a waste of time. Your most important search parameter is where you want to live.

3. **Get a list of *all* the potential employers in each location,** whether they have posted job listings or not. It is easy. On your search engine, type in the location with the words 'business directory', 'laboratory', 'small business directory', or a similar phrase that relates to the kind of work you seek. 'Edinburgh Business Directory', used as a search term, will give you information no job-listing site will come close to.

4. **Find out about organizations that appeal to you,** whether or not they have advertised open positions.

5. **Get up close and personal.** Check the companies' websites to see what jobs are listed, if any. If you find a listing that matches your qualifications, *don't* respond immediately. Find a more personal means of access: with a few phone calls you can get the name of a person in the company (not necessarily in a recruitment role) who is connected to that position or knows someone whose job is related to it.

With this step-by-step approach you are taking more time and being more deliberate than if you simply relied upon the hit-or-miss routine of the commercial job-search sites and CV broadcasting.

In following this strategy you are not relying on a flawed system of overhyped job-finding services to manage your future. You are skillfully managing your career and your job search on your own terms.

4

Discovering and Communicating Your Strengths

The Tyranny of Job Titles and Descriptions

B efore you make use of the various approaches to transmitting your qualifications to the right employers, you need to formulate what's best and most marketable about you and get this into language that communicates it well. There are two aspects to this: job titles and strengths. Job titles are about assigned *functions* or *duties*. Strengths show your inherent ability to produce *results*. Strengths cannot be assigned: you have them already and just need to clarify and apply them. A perfect CV will acknowledge the job title – if there is one – and drive home your ability to produce results inside of this.

A job title tends to be a rigid construct whose dimensions are copied from old manuals, HR compensation systems, or past job postings. Descriptions for general and well-used titles such as Editor, Researcher, and Designer don't say much to begin with; others that are more specific – such as Search Engine Optimizer, Training Design Specialist, and Fitness Instructor – are clearer. However, in the fluid environment of business, jobs change in character, structure, and emphasis as fast as their organizations change strategies to respond to new challenges – almost yearly.

Because you will see job titles and descriptions on websites, in classified ads, and in many other contexts, you can't ignore them. However, if you are going after such a job, when you know more about the company you can get beyond their words and respond with a bit more uniqueness, as we mentioned in the information on the hidden job market.

For example, I have for years produced software related to career development, CVs, and performance. From time to time I get CVs and e-mails from programmers and website designers. Only one in twenty-five has taken the time to do enough basic research (calling in advance, going to my website, finding a book I have written) to find out about my interests and concerns. Those who connect their skills to my needs, even in basic ways, are guaranteed at least a phone interview.

> Peter Carpenter, Recruiter: *I am often amazed at how people present themselves. They instinctively go right to their last job title or description. I'm a pretty basic interviewer. I have their CV in front of me, and I start the conversation by saying simply, 'So, Pat, tell me about yourself.' Mostly what I hear next is a recital of what Pat did in her last job, or the job before that, or at college. So I ask myself, what does that have to do with us – here, now, tomorrow? I know the job titles are similar – our automated tracking system took care of that – but does she know what our products are? Does she know our industry, and the skills and aptitudes we need now? I have to dig out the strong points. We are so keyworded in our approach that it becomes like a crossword puzzle. I'm impressed when a person can speak not only about the processes, about the roles and responsibilities they held, but also about the results they produced, where they held on to a project when it was in trouble, something about their personal values, leadership, motivation.*
>
> *I want to know about the skills and qualities that go beyond the work they have done so far, or even their ideas for the future of our business. I think it starts with their CV. People try to fit in what they think is expected and get formal and mechanical in their thinking. They don't think it through much.*

Know Your Strengths and Communicate Them

Your strengths are your most successful, marketable, and productive qualities. Although experience helps to define them, they also exist and can be used if your actual job experience is limited. They multiply the value of the skills and specialties that show up as keywords. Compare: *I excel at using Photoshop* with *Design print-ready fashion photo layouts for publishers using Photoshop*. 'Photoshop' would definitely be a keyword in either case; however, readers will see more when they read or hear what you did with the skill.

The Perfect CV helps you build a database of valuable strengths with terms and phrases to use as building blocks. These terms and phrases can be used in your CVs, covering letters, interviews, follow-ups, and personal planning. Combined, they form your real net worth, a dictionary of your market value. Acquaint yourself with the categories of strengths that follow, and then in Part Two, Your CV Workout, see how they line up with your work to enhance your power vocabulary. This process of promoting your best gives you a competitive edge.

Do others inventory their strengths? Not often. Communicate them well? Rarely. It would take another book to explain the phenomenon of people not being able to communicate what is really great about them. In a commercial environment this doesn't make much sense; companies always boost what they do in a way that makes them most attractive to their customers. You should too. At the least you should know what you want to communicate that makes the most of your best. If you haven't thought it through, you can't communicate it. So assembling the message comes first, before delivering it.

If you don't know what to say when someone asks, 'Why should I hire you?' you won't be hired.

If you were a car – say, a Mercedes – there would be a number of terms to define your various capabilities and appeal. If you were a solicitor, you would have hundreds of terms at your fingertips to win your case. You can gain the same type of advantage by learning stronger ways to distinguish yourself and communicate your strengths. Work with the terms that follow. On these pages you are gaining familiarity with categories of strengths: in order to start exercising self-esteem, you need to speak out loud about your own strong points. Part

Two includes exercises for you to flesh out the specific terms that apply to you.

Categories of Strengths

Know-how That which you know how to do well. Many of us take our know-how for granted and then forget to speak about it in the stress of an interview or when faced with putting words to paper. *Example: I know how to motivate people to dare to take risks.* Know-how is the application of a number of skills. HR types would call these 'competencies'.

Skills Sets of acquired learning: calculus, welding, flying, book-keeping, programming. More precise than know-how, these accumulate from learning, practice, and training. Sets of skills are combined with experience to form job titles or even job descriptions.

Accomplishments The results you have produced. They are best stated in terms of outcomes, not sets of activities. Activities are what you do; outcomes are the pay-offs. *Examples: I cut processing time by 20 per cent. I improved employee retention significantly. Working as a team, we became the leading national distributor of our product.*

Capabilities The potential of your skills to create accomplishments. Capabilities show what you can do in the future, whether or not you have done the same exact thing in the past. (See the targeted CV format in Chapter 6.) When you use a capability statement, especially when you have done your research in advance, the interviewer's mind is pulled towards you. It is a bold and successful way to speak to what the employer wants and needs rather than what you have already done, although the conversation will soon require you to back up your assertions and sell your capability. By introducing what is probably on the shopping list of the employer, you have got the attention where you want it. *Examples: I can help you build a successful sales campaign that doesn't require discounting. I can increase security and confidentiality in the payroll process.*

Personal Qualities The attributes that define your personality, character, and style, such as persistence, creativity, integrity, humour, trustworthiness, leadership, logical thinking, being a fast learner. These are intangible yet important, especially in matching the cultural needs of an organization. Be aware of your qualities and include them in your CV and covering letter with an eye on the job you are seeking. Because these statements are usually not quantified and are self-defined, they are frequently given lower significance in straight CV screening, and definitely in the scanning and tracking process. (See the section on keywords below.) However, they do count, and by using them strategically – especially in the interview process – you can score the extra points that will get you over the goal line. Knowing your personal qualities can sometimes help you fill in an interview question. *Example: Interviewer – Are you familiar with the XR7Q calculating process? You – Not yet. However, I am a fast learner.*

Passions What you feel excited about or personally dedicated to doing; your strongest interests. This is another important intangible for you and for future employers. It's most helpful in the covering letter and interview as long as you know that the employer's objective is not to satisfy your interests. Being clear about your interests counts most when you can demonstrate that what you have done is consistent with them. Employers want motivated people as much as they want talent. To get both is the goal. *Example: 'Not only did the project exceed expectations, it was also gratifying to see the bottom-line results of my dedication to customer satisfaction.'*

What You Value

Personal qualities relate directly to your values (what is important to you in all aspects of your life). By clarifying and prioritizing what you value, you can better judge the work or culture that will satisfy you in the future. A good question to ask in a phone exploration or interview is 'What are your company's values?' **Examples** Personal values: collaboration, lifetime learning, open communication, integrity, risk-taking, flexibility. Company values: shareholder value, taking care of customers, innovation, adherence to rules, seniority, non-hierarchical structure. Part Two, Your CV Workout, will give you a chance to look at these.

Keywords and phrases After you have learned to articulate your strengths, you will need to combine them with words and phrases that are search-engine recognizable in the body of your CV or in a summary statement. This is essential where recruiters sort and search CVs electronically or use applicant tracking systems and Internet job banks. If the main shopped-for terms do not show up, your CV will not be retrieved electronically.

Buzzwords and Keywords

Keywords and Phrases

If you send a CV by e-mail or post to a medium-sized or large employer, the CV may be scanned into a database with thousands of others, sorted by keywords and phrases, and, if your keywords exactly match what the employer has listed, possibly reviewed by recruiters or screeners looking for precise matches. Given the number of candidates with similar keywords or combinations of keywords, you will be ranked by potential. The actual ranking is done differently by various systems used: some will measure the number of times a key skill is mentioned; others will determine how close the keyword is to the top of the CV; and others will have other protocols, which change regularly. If you are in a high-demand category, and your keywords reflect that, more attention will be paid to that aspect of your CV. (Keep in mind that these systems were designed by tech types, so the use of searchable terms denoting overly precise skills – characteristic of science and technology – is not surprising.)

Most job titles are made up of a variety of skills and experience. This is why it is so important that you know about the firms you are most interested in and construct a CV responding to their interests and needs. Your CV may describe more accurately what is needed than does the company's own posted description. Caution: if you are planning to use digital services as an introduction to a potential employer rather than starting with human contact, read the job description and others like it from the same company before you build your keyword list.

Conflicting agendas in the hiring organizations often foster a muddled approach to employment. On the one hand, they want to find skillful people who are flexible and mobile, who can look in new directions to discern what customers want, who can bring new life to old organizational structures. They want *talent*. On the other hand, for reasons of economy and efficiency and the enormous volume of input from CV broadcasters, they turn to keyword search engines that make individuality harder to find. Todd Raphael, publisher of the American HR information website Workforce.com, put it this way: 'I guess you could say that the process of finding a way through or around the filtration barriers is part of the game. The ones who get through show qualities of imagination and perseverance that the ones who get stopped don't.'

Recruiters use keyword screening as a way to reduce the number of CVs they must sort through in a market where there are hundreds of thousands of (often mismatched or out-of-date) candidate CVs for each position. This flood of data is greatly exacerbated by the scores of CV spamming services that charge anxious job seekers for sending CVs to 'thousands of employers and recruiters'. Search engines are used to slice and dice gigabytes of data and filter in or filter out people by the keywords and phrases they use in their CVs or online profiles. From a talented job seeker's perspective, automatic electronic filtering by keywords and phrases can make designing a well-balanced CV for a range of possible opportunities a chore unless you understand thoroughly how it works, and are willing to use strategies that take you out of the filtration machinery.

One top recruiter of long-term health care personnel sees this as a benefit of significant proportions that allows him to specify the exact qualifications, degrees, and experience he needs from applicants. On the other hand, he says, 'I am lucky the people we look for have measurable skill sets and legally mandated qualifications, so we can keep our criteria clean and neat. I worry about firms who need more variety and scope in their hiring. I'm not sure I would have even got seen if the system had been in place when they hired me. What my job requires isn't definable!'

Here are two ways keywords are used by job seekers and employers in digital job searches:

1. To search one of the many job boards, you enter one or more keywords in the 'search jobs' section and retrieve the names of employers who listed jobs with these terms. With some services like Monster.com, you can do this for free even if you haven't signed up for a membership. This is a fast way to get details about these companies: postal and e-mail addresses, and other listed jobs. Since there are thousands of job boards, some general and some special-purpose, you should identify which job boards are most relevant first. Using your favourite Internet search engine, add a specialty or field after 'job boards', and find those closest to your area of interest. (For example, 'job boards civil engineers'.)

2. You may enter a CV into a 'CV data bank', available on most job boards, and it will be held in storage for future job searches. Since you are not the active searcher, be sure the CV you post has all the potential keywords and phrases for which you want it retrieved. The language of your CV should be precise and include functional, technical, and professional terms related to your job target. A searchable summary statement is recommended for this. See page 92 for more information about summary statements. *Note: if you have two or three different job targets and different employers to send CVs to, prepare different objective and summary statements for each.*

Here is an extract from a CV in Part Six. Notice the words (italicized) that qualify as keywords or phrases that can be searched.

PART OBJECTIVE:

Instructor of *Food Service Management* to *develop food service workers'* skills, improve *restaurant quality*, and increase *customer loyalty*.

SUMMARY:

- *Chef* with *business, catering, and event management* experience.

- Skilled in *staff development*, including *kitchen skills, sanitation, customer service*, and *employee motivation*.

- *Restored profitability* to a small, specialized menu restaurant.

- *Supervisory experience* with a major *hotel chain*.

PART TWO

Your CV Workout

*P*roducing a CV means translating what's best about you into a form that communicates this to potential employers. Its aim is to attract their interest in meeting you and discussing opportunities. Very few of us have ever had or taken the opportunity to focus on our talents, strengths, and accomplishments in a literal way, and you may need help choosing the right terms, identifying personal priorities, and writing statements that communicate what you offer to others. The forms in this part will help you. Use as many of these worksheets as you can regardless of your level of experience.

Take time to focus on what's best about yourself. Don't hesitate to speak well of what you have done, just as an employer would speak well of their company and products. Think of your future and how you can work when you are operating at peak performance.

INSTRUCTIONS:

1. First, read briefly through all the pages in this part so you know where we are going.

2. Start with the CV Readiness Section and indicate which areas you are interested in working on.

3. Take enough time with each section to uncover information that is relevant even if not immediately apparent.

4. Go back over the material later to find places where you can upgrade or improve. Share the process with another person who knows you well.

CV Readiness

What I want to work on:

Instructions: There are a number of assessments you can select in this CV Workout. Tick the columns corresponding to your needs to:	I want to work on this	I don't want to work on this	I'm not sure
Define work interests			
Profile success factors			
Profile values			
Write a selling case			
Profile work successes			
Write talent statements and keywords			
Select work functions			
Identify skills			
Select job possibilities			
Set up job targets			

My salary target is: £_____ per month

My minimum is: £_____ per month

What I need to demonstrate in my CV to prove I am worth my salary target is:

_____

_____

In my view, what turns a good CV into a great CV is:

_____

_____

_____

A person who can help me produce (review, edit) my CV is:

_____

Your Work Interests

A job that works for you is one that combines both your skills and your interests. Stimulating interests have a place in the work of your future and will contribute to your productivity and the quality of your life.

INSTRUCTIONS:
Tick each interest that applies to you – add to the following list as you wish.

I (would) like:

____ making deals

____ teaching/training

____ computers

____ resolving disputes

____ travel

____ variety

____ restoring things

____ consulting

____ sales work

____ research

____ supervising

____ taking care of others

____ coaching

____ learning new things

____ making videos

____ music

____ family counselling

____ making presentations

____ writing

____ organizing complexity

____ being outdoors

____ solving problems

____ negotiating

____ interviewing

____ politics

____ working with numbers

____ sports

____ public service

____ producing events

____ working with my hands

____ routine

____ working on my own

____ working with ideas

____ cooking and catering

____ taking risks

____ creative work

____ designing systems

____ public appearances

____ conducting meetings

____ analysing

____ challenging goals

____ intricate work

____ leading a team

Add more interests below:

Considering the interests you have selected and any modifications or additions, list those you would most like to see reflected in your next job.

_____   _____

_____   _____

There are many work styles to choose from: working from home, part time, consulting, lots of travel, little travel, job sharing, temp service, and more. List your preferred work styles below:

_____   _____

_____   _____

Basic Success Factors

Past successes of all kinds – school, community, and family – are indicators of things you were good at and enjoyed accomplishing.

INSTRUCTIONS:

1. Look over the situations in the left-hand column and tick those that remind you of a success you are proud of.

2. Write short statements describing the behaviours (actions) and qualities (principles, beliefs, motivations) behind these successes. **Example:** I successfully put together a local business leaders' forum to discuss community issues. It took persistence and organization to get it started and keep it going.

☐ A successful event at school

☐ A successful event in my community

☐ A success I achieved in a particularly challenging situation

☐ A financial success I am proud of

☐ An important team success

☐ A successful project I furthered

☐ Something I successfully learned how to do

☐ An entrepreneurial success

☐ A time when I successfully took a risk

I successfully: _____

_____

_____

I successfully: _____

_____

_____

I successfully: _____

_____

_____

I successfully: _____

_____

_____

Summarize the personal *qualities* behind these successes and list them below, e.g., my dogged persistence, my ability to collaborate, my imagination, etc.

QUALITIES THAT MOST CONTRIBUTE TO MY SUCCESS ARE:

My_____

My_____

My_____

My_____

Your Values

A value is a characteristic or trait that is important to you for its own sake – as an end, not a means to an end. When priorities change, some values get sidetracked or forgotten. It is useful in a transition of lifestyle or work style to inventory your values afresh and adjust your priorities.

INSTRUCTIONS:

1. Read all the values in both lists.

2. Tick – in the YES column – five values in each list that are most important to you.

3. Tick the boxes on the right to indicate which values you want to focus on more.

YES	I Most Value	Focus more on this	OK as it is	YES	I Most Value	Focus more on this	OK as it is
	Home and family				Success and recognition		
	Money				How I use my time		
	Learning				Teaching		
	Giving				Saving money		
	Managing other people				Leading		
	Physicality				Mental stimulation		
	My feelings				Paying attention to feelings		
	Flexibility				Security		
	Trust				Loyalty		
	Innovation				Consistency		
	Planning in advance				Reacting quickly		
	Being myself				Solving puzzles		
	Keeping deadlines				Keeping commitments		
	Ordinary work				Unconventional work		
	Goal orientation				Imagination		
	Budgeting well				Nonconformity		
	Communicating				Making presentations		
	Coaching others				Being coached		
	Structure				Flexibility and versatility		
	Add other values:				Add other values:		

4. Combine terms from the qualities list (facing page) and the values you selected above to describe yourself in a 'Selling Case' paragraph (a concise paragraph that encapsulates what's best about you). In the space below respond to an interviewer who just said, 'Tell me about yourself.' _____

_____

_____

_____

_____

_____

Successes at Work

In this worksheet you will assess the most relevant (to your future) successes at specific work assignments – part time, full time, voluntary or school projects, and undertakings. Later you will select which to use in your next CV.

INSTRUCTIONS:

1. Identify work situations starting with the most recent. You may repeat the employer to include several successes.

2. Express the successes you accomplished in each work role by listing tangible results you produced and how they benefitted your employer. Keep the material short; you will come back to it for expansion later.

1. Date: _____

    Employer/other: _____

    Your title: _____

    Result successfully accomplished: _____

    _____

    _____

    Benefit/payoff: _____

    _____

    Skills and qualities employed: _____

    _____

    _____

2. Date: _____

    Employer/other: _____

    Your title: _____

    Result successfully accomplished: _____

    _____

    _____

    Benefit/payoff: _____

    _____

    Skills and qualities employed: _____

    _____

    _____

3. Date: _____

    Employer/other: _____

    Your title: _____

    Result successfully accomplished: _____

    _____

    _____

    Benefit/payoff: _____

    _____

    Skills and qualities employed: _____

    _____

    _____

4. Date: _____

    Employer/other: _____

    Your title: _____

    Result successfully accomplished: _____

    _____

    _____

    Benefit/payoff: _____

    _____

    Skills and qualities employed: _____

    _____

    _____

4. Successes at Work
(continued)

3. Based on what you have expressed about yourself so far, in the space below write statements about yourself that reflect your strengths. Consider it a practice run.

I consider myself to be strong at:

_____

_____

_____

_____

_____

_____

_____

_____

I also consider myself to be a strong:

_____

_____

_____

_____

_____

_____

_____

_____

My most marketable strength is my:

_____

_____

_____

_____

_____

_____

_____

_____

Talent Prompts

Action Words

Used effectively, active verbs take your CV's reader right to the point. This lets you shorten your statements into brief bulleted lists of capability. The statement 'I was responsible for performing department-wide audits' becomes simply: 'performed department audits'.

INSTRUCTIONS:

1. Read the list of active verbs below. Add terms as necessary.

2. Tick all those you might use in constructing statements about your achievements.

3. Choose five to ten of those you checked that suggest what you have achieved in past work that could apply to future work. List them in the right-hand column.

Administered	Delivered	Instituted	Provided	
Advised	Designed	Instructed	Purchased	_____
Analysed	Detected	Interpreted	Realized	
Arbitrated	Determined	Interviewed	Received	_____
Arranged	Developed	Invented	Recommended	
Assembled	Devised	Lectured	Recorded	_____
Assisted	Diagnosed	Logged	Reduced (losses)	
Audited	Directed	Maintained	Referred	_____
Built	Discovered	Managed	Rendered	
Calculated	Dispensed	Navigated	Represented	_____
Charted	Disproved	Negotiated	Researched	
Collected	Distributed	Obtained	Restored	_____
Communicated	Drew up	Operated	Reviewed	
Completed	Edited	Ordered	Routed	_____
Compounded	Eliminated	Organized	Selected	
Conducted	Evaluated	Oversaw	Served	_____
Conserved	Examined	Performed	Sold	
Consolidated	Expanded	Planned	Solved	_____
Constructed	Formulated	Prepared	Studied	
Consulted	Founded	Prescribed	Supervised	_____
Controlled	Identified	Presented	Supplied	
Coordinated	Implemented	Processed	Tested	
Corresponded	Improved	Produced	Trained	
Counselled	Increased	Promoted	Translated	
Created	Installed	Protected	Wrote	

Talent Statements

No matter what CV format or method of delivery you use, you must express your talents and experience in words and phrases that communicate value. You have already defined **qualities** and **values** behind your successes on pages 42 and 43. On page 54 you will define **results** you can produce for a prospective employer, and then on page 48 you will transform specific **skills** and **functions** into keywords and phrases that can be used in an electronic job search.

INSTRUCTIONS:

1. In the spaces below, use the action words and personal qualities you listed in previous exercises to construct statements that demonstrate your talents. Use a format similar to the example below if you wish to.

2. Write as many Talent Statements as you can, using additional paper if needed. These Talent Statements will be a very helpful first step in formulating and customizing your CVs and covering letters and in selecting keywords to use.

Value   Keywords

I profitably administered *pension fund allocations* by collaborating with others.

    Active verb   Success quality

_____

_____

_____

_____

_____

_____

_____

_____

_____

Ready to Deliver

Functions Performed

A job function is a recognizable category of work assignment or benefit you provide to an employer. The function is broader than a specific job title (*1998–2004: Manager of Web Design, Cisco Systems*), which is rooted in time and connected to a particular employer. In contrast to this title, the function 'web design' could be present in many different jobs or experiences and not carry a title. A person may have been involved in planning and designing websites as part of their work as a catalogue sales manager, or as an assistant curator in a museum. The sum of this person's experience in web design might be substantial and could qualify them for a position, but since it was never a job title it won't show up as a heading in a chronological CV, and they could lose out to someone with less skill who has the job title at the top of a CV.

In a functional CV (see page 71 for example) you organize selected parts of your capability into functional categories and show these on your CV in an order most relevant to the jobs you are after. You can change the order to emphasize the functions most relevant to any employer or position.

There are hundreds of functional heading possibilities. The purpose of this worksheet is to prepare a list of relevant functions in advance so when you want to consider doing a functional CV you can choose those that relate most to the job target you are going for.

Here is a list of sample functional headings:

- Budgeting
- Editing
- Strategic planning
- Risk management
- Quality control
- Training
- Managing projects
- Software design
- Market research
- Financial planning
- Network programming
- Graphic design
- Scheduling
- Cost control

Using the list on the left as a model, think of at least five functional headings you could use that define areas of your expertise. List them below:

_____

_____

_____

_____

_____

_____

_____

_____

Ready to Deliver

Know-how, Skills, and Specialties

Frequently when people sit down in front of a keyboard and a blank screen to compose their CVs a kind of writer's block shows up, and they can't easily recall the skills and know-how they have learned and used in past occupations, training, and informal pursuits. If you take the time to work this out in advance, and perhaps come back to it a couple of times, your CV will be much easier to write.

INSTRUCTIONS:

In the spaces below take time to inventory specific know-how, skills, and specialties. List whatever you think of, as one idea will lead to the next and suggest something else that is worth remembering later when you are writing your perfect CV. Use extra paper as needed and insert it in the book. Read over the earlier worksheets to remind yourself of your strengths. Pull your ideas together in powerful language.

I am a skilled (chef, underwriter, editor):

_____

_____

_____

_____

_____

_____

_____

_____

I know how to (list below) better than most:

_____

_____

_____

_____

_____

_____

_____

_____

I can competently operate (name equipment, processes, computer programs, procedures):

_____

_____

_____

_____

_____

_____

_____

I have studied/learned/been certified/specialized in:

_____

_____

_____

_____

_____

_____

_____

_____

Job Families

A Job Family is a category of work within which there are literally hundreds of different jobs. Although the tendency is to look back at specific jobs or industries (or specializations) with which you are familiar, it is a good idea to explore new applications for your talent and strengths. Even in the same industry new job situations are being invented daily. Soon you will choose two or three job targets to direct your CVs towards. Use these worksheets to expand your choices.

INSTRUCTIONS:

1. Review the list of Job Families below. Draw a line through each that you are sure you wouldn't want to be involved in.

2. Circle those you would be interested in at least exploring – adding any that are missing.

3. Then select five of the circled job families and transfer them to the Job Family lists on pages 52 and 53.

Insurance	Banking	Human Resources
Entrepreneurial	Politics	Computer Design
Materials	Retailing	Sales
Journalism	Finance	Consulting
Industrial Design	Agriculture	Property
Commercial Arts	Communications	Information Technology
Education	Marketing	Travel and Leisure
Publishing	Security	Personal Services
Food Services	Health Care	Customer Services
Entertainment	Children's Services	Sports
Fashion	Economics	Legal
Interior Design	Government	Engineering
Construction	Criminology	Internet
Consumer Electronics	Environmental Protection	Career Services
Transport	Accounting	Car Industry
List additional Job Families below.		

Job Possibilities

Each of the Job Families you have selected from the list on page 50 has hundreds of job types and functions connected to it. We call these Job Possibilities. The titles of these are constantly changing as technology and business practices evolve. Brainstorm just one Job Family, say Car Industry, and you will see that there are hundreds of Job Possibilities, from designing cars, selling, manufacturing, financing, repairing, teaching, safety, hiring, writing about, advertising, budgeting, to research and more. In less than fifteen minutes on the Internet you could find scores of Job Possibilities in any Job Family. By expanding your thinking about the field your list will grow to include many possibilities that relate to your skills and interests and dozens that don't. Some that seem irrelevant will suggest others that are good matches.

INSTRUCTIONS:

1. Review the five Job Families you selected in the previous exercise and placed in the boxes on page 52. You can change, add, or substitute later using additional paper if you wish to further expand your choices. Think about the field as broadly as possible and brainstorm as many possible jobs as you can think of or find on the Internet for each Job Family.

2. Under each of the selected Job Family headings list Job Possibilities – from your brainstorming – that might be right for you. Try to come up with ten or more possibilities for each Job Family.

3. When you have listed your Job Possibilities, take time to review, add, or modify, as you measure yourself against them, and put ticks alongside those that appeal to you most. Don't worry about getting the titles right – you can change them at any time.

4. Of the possibilities you've ticked transfer your top five choices to the Job Targets box and assess them. In the Values and Skills columns, rate how each job would reflect your ideals by placing an H for high, M for medium, or L for low. Then rank your choices by number, with the most desirable job as number one. The top three are your Job Targets for now. We will explore them on the next few pages.

Job Possibilities
(continued)

Selected Job Family:

_____

Job Family Possiblities:

1.	6.
2.	7.
3.	8.
4.	9.
5.	10.

Selected Job Family:

_____

Job Family Possiblities:

1.	6.
2.	7.
3.	8.
4.	9.
5.	10.

Selected Job Family:

_____

Job Family Possiblities:

1.	6.
2.	7.
3.	8.
4.	9.
5.	10.

Job Possibilities
(continued)

Selected Job Family:

_____

Job Family Possiblities:

1.	6.
2.	7.
3.	8.
4.	9.
5.	10.

Selected Job Family:

_____

Job Family Possiblities:

1.	6.
2.	7.
3.	8.
4.	9.
5.	10.

Job Targets	Values	Skills	Rank
1.			
2.			
3.			
4.			
5.			

Job Target No. 1

OUTCOMES AND RESULTS

Your No. 1 Job Target: _____

What industry or industries is it most closely associated with? _____

_____

What would an employer be looking for most from someone in this job? *(Note: answer this now if you are reasonably clear about the nature of the job, or after you have done the research you need in order to be more specific. See page 114 for research recommended to customize your CV.)*

The ability to:

_____

_____

_____

INSTRUCTIONS:

Reviewing your work on pages 40–53 and your own knowledge of yourself, what are the particular *outcomes* or *results* you are confident you can produce for an employer in this job-target field related to what you listed above?

I am confident of my ability to produce: _____

_____

_____

_____

I am confident of my ability to produce: _____

_____

_____

_____

I am confident of my ability to produce: _____

_____

_____

_____

* Outcomes and Results = tangible accomplishments, deliverables, measurable pay-offs. Example: *A fully documented user's manual for customers.*

Job Target No. 1

POWER PARAGRAPHS

Here you will summarize, from the previous pages, the most important material to include in your CV for Job Target No. 1. You can do this now or wait until later if you want to do more research on particular employer candidates. When you assemble your final CV all of this information will be useful.

1. Rewrite the Selling Case paragraph on page 43 to fit this Job Target specifically.

   Tell me about yourself:

   _____

   _____

   _____

   _____

   _____

2. Review your Strengths on pages 42 and 49 and list those most relevant to this Job Target.

3. Review your Talent Statements on page 47 and select or rewrite one expressly for this Job Target.

   _____

   _____

   _____

   _____

4. Review your Ready to Deliver material on page 48 and list items that support this Job Target.

Job Target No. 2

OUTCOMES AND RESULTS

Your No. 2 Job Target: _____

What industry or industries is it most closely associated with? _____

_____

What would an employer be looking for most from someone in this job?

The ability to:

_____

_____

_____

INSTRUCTIONS:

Reviewing your work on pages 40–53 and your own knowledge of yourself, what are the particular *outcomes* or *results* you are confident you can produce for an employer in this job-target field related to what you listed above?

I am confident of my ability to produce: _____

_____

_____

_____

_____

I am confident of my ability to produce: _____

_____

_____

_____

_____

I am confident of my ability to produce: _____

_____

_____

_____

_____

Job Target No. 2
POWER PARAGRAPHS

Here you will summarize, from the previous pages, the most important material to include in your CV for Job Target No. 2. You can do this now or wait until later if you want to do more research on particular employer candidates. When you assemble your final CV all of this information will be useful.

1. Rewrite the Selling Case paragraph on page 43 to fit this Job Target specifically.

   Tell me about yourself:

   _____

   _____

   _____

   _____

   _____

2. Review your Strengths on pages 42 and 49 and list those most relevant to this Job Target.

3. Review your Talent Statements on page 47 and select or rewrite one expressly for this Job Target.

   _____

   _____

   _____

   _____

4. Review your Ready to Deliver material on page 48 and list items that support this Job Target.

Job Target No. 3

Your No. 3 Job Target: _____

What industry or industries is it most closely associated with? _____

_____

What would an employer be looking for most from someone in this job?

The ability to:

_____

_____

_____

INSTRUCTIONS:

Reviewing your work on pages 40–53 and your own knowledge of yourself, what are the particular *outcomes* or *results* you are confident you can produce for an employer in this job-target field related to what you listed above?

I am confident of my ability to produce: _____

_____

_____

_____

_____

I am confident of my ability to produce: _____

_____

_____

_____

_____

I am confident of my ability to produce: _____

_____

_____

_____

_____

Make each Job Target carry its own powerful message about the variety of your talent.

Job Target No. 3
POWER PARAGRAPHS

Here you will summarize, from the previous pages, the most important material to include in your CV for Job Target No. 3. You can do this now or wait until later if you want to do more research on particular employer candidates. When you assemble your final CV all of this information will be useful.

1. Rewrite the Selling Case paragraph on page 43 to fit this Job Target specifically.

    Tell me about yourself:

    _____

    _____

    _____

    _____

    _____

2. Review your Strengths on pages 42 and 49 and list those most relevant to this Job Target.

3. Review your Talent Statements on page 47 and select or rewrite one expressly for this Job Target.

    _____

    _____

    _____

    _____

4. Review your Ready to Deliver material on page 48 and list items that support this Job Target.

Building Your Perfect CVs

*N*ow that you've assembled the raw material of your perfect CV you can decide which CV formats, organization types, and layouts will best fit your situation and most appeal to the employers who reflect your Job Targets.

If you skipped Part Two and already know what you want to say on your CV, you will still learn how selecting the right formats is important for you. After you have selected your format and style, you can go right to the CV and covering letter samples in Parts Five and Six. Use anything in the book that can strengthen your ability to take charge of your future.

Contents of Part Three

6

Perfect CV Formats

CV Preparation Guidelines

Before we describe the formats you can use, review these basic CV preparation principles and tips:

A presentation CV is produced to look terrific when printed. You need them for interviews (take two copies along), to give to others who will send them to friends, and for the companies that do not yet use electronic CV tracking services. Also use the presentation form for high-level positions that will usually not be in the regular system. Most of the sample CVs and covering letters in this book are shown in presentation form.

A digital CV is a presentation CV that has been converted carefully into ASCII or plain text, and is distributed in this standard electronic messaging format. It loses most of the layout features of the presentation version – bold and italic type, font styles, bullets, underlining, centring, and more. You learn to make the conversion later in this chapter.

The Selling Case

Every CV is a sales document in that you – the product and sales person combined – are offering a tangible value to a potential customer: an employer in this case. Regardless of format, style, and layout, if your sales message is not clear, your CV will probably not get you hired. Your Selling Case is your fundamental one-paragraph pitch for employers (see p. 43). It must be embedded in your consciousness as you work on your actual CV. The rule of thumb to follow is that everything on your CV is part of a communication that answers the question: 'Why should I hire you?'

A good way to prepare your Selling Case is by using the past to support what you will accomplish in the future. Here is one model showing how the logic might go:

> Using my (skills and qualities), aided by my (education), I am able to produce (measurable results) for you by doing (activities) as part of my role as (job title or function) with your firm.

You can put the elements and their connections together in a variety of ways, but try practising this model first:

Using my _____

Aided by my _____

I am able to produce _____

For you by _____

As part of my role as _____ with your firm.

Length

Keep your CV short. It is a selection document, not a hiring document. If written and edited well, a one- or two-page CV (preferably one) is sufficient to describe almost anyone's best capabilities – at least as a lead-in to a more detailed presentation in person or by phone. At the interview you have the opportunity to fill in many details. The reader's mind can absorb and remember more information when it is on one page or one screen than when it's spread across many. Focus your CV on the key points needed to gain a recruiter's attention and offer more detailed information on request. Your CV should cover in detail the most relevant and recent parts of your work experience. Anything beyond the past ten years can be condensed to a few lines, unless it has a special significance for your current job target. Minimize personal details.

The Formats

In the following pages we review four different CV formats. Each presentation includes a description of the format and its pros and cons, the instructions for preparing that format, and a sample CV written in that format. The four formats are:

Chronological CV – most commonly used, easy to read and write. It shows your most recent experience first and is good for demonstrating continuity.

Functional CV – headlines the functions you've performed that relate most to the job you are seeking, regardless of when you performed them. Chronology takes second place. If you have been out of work for some time, or are entering the formal job market for the first time, this format will reduce the impact of that. This format is also useful for those who are changing fields.

Targeted CV – an unconventional format that looks forwards and stresses what you can achieve for a company. What you can do takes precedence over what you have done. It requires good research about the employer you are aiming it at.

CV Alternative – a letter substituting for a formal CV. It works best for people who have a special situation that takes some explaining, such as returning army personnel or someone who has been bringing up children full time and wants to re-enter the job market.

The Chronological CV

This format is popular with employers because it is the easiest to read, the most compatible with search sites, and the easiest to rank. The chronological CV tells, in a compact way, the history of your work experience to date. It starts with the present, then goes back in reverse chronology to what you have been doing since you left school or further education. It emphasizes your current or most recent work over work you have done before. Usually as much as 30 per cent of the CV is focused on the most recent experience.

Unfortunately, the chronological format can work against you if you don't want to stay on the same job track as the one listed at the top of your CV. The recruiter may do a 'fast scan' – read the headline only – and use that to decide whether to read further. If you are interested in a new direction or if your last job was something you took just to tide you over, you will want to use a different format.

PREPARING A CHRONOLOGICAL CV:

- Start with your present or most recent position and work backwards in time, devoting the most space to your most recent employment. This looks best if there are relatively few time gaps and employment changes.

- Cover just the last fifteen years or three or four positions held. Summarize older positions simply and briefly, even if they are related to your present targeted work. One-line descriptions are sufficient and could be put under the heading 'Other Relevant Experience'.

- Include the relevant keywords a company search engine might look for. (You might want to change this for different employer targets.) Keywords can be shown in the body of the CV (as in the example opposite) or in a summary statement (see page 92).

- In your job history, cite years, not months and days, for experience with different employers. You can provide exact detail on dates on a formal application form.

- It's not necessary to list every position held in an organization. Provide more detail for those most relevant to your targeted job.

Chronological CV

Bold texts look good on a presentation CV but will get lost when digitized

Should eliminate '/' so each term will register when scanned

E-mail a must

Emphasizes long-term employment

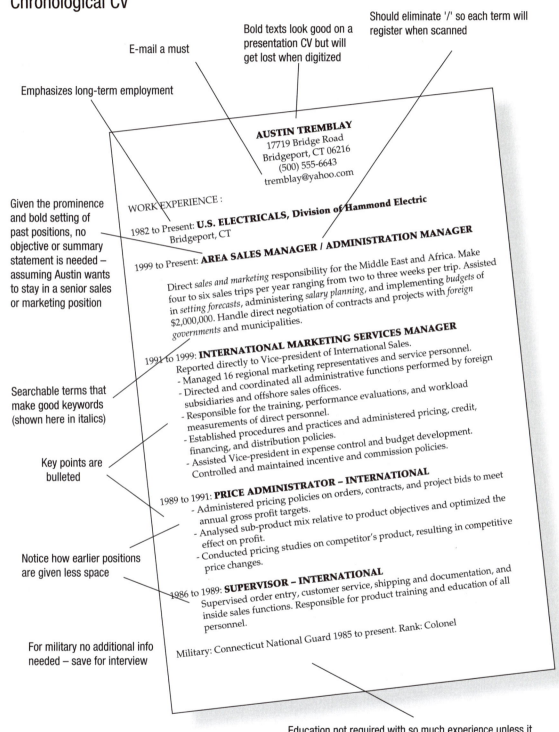

AUSTIN TREMBLAY
17719 Bridge Road
Bridgeport, CT 06216
(500) 555-6643
tremblay@yahoo.com

WORK EXPERIENCE :

1982 to Present: **U.S. ELECTRICALS, Division of Hammond Electric**
Bridgeport, CT

1999 to Present: **AREA SALES MANAGER / ADMINISTRATION MANAGER**

Direct *sales* and *marketing* responsibility for the Middle East and Africa. Make four to six sales trips per year ranging from two to three weeks per trip. Assisted in *setting forecasts*, administering *salary planning*, and implementing *budgets* of $2,000,000. Handle direct negotiation of contracts and projects with *foreign governments* and municipalities.

1991 to 1999: **INTERNATIONAL MARKETING SERVICES MANAGER**
Reported directly to Vice-president of International Sales.
- Managed 16 regional marketing representatives and service personnel.
- Directed and coordinated all administrative functions performed by foreign subsidiaries and offshore sales offices.
- Responsible for the training, performance evaluations, and workload measurements of direct personnel.
- Established procedures and practices and administered pricing, credit, financing, and distribution policies.
- Assisted Vice-president in expense control and budget development. Controlled and maintained incentive and commission policies.

1989 to 1991: **PRICE ADMINISTRATOR – INTERNATIONAL**
- Administered pricing policies on orders, contracts, and project bids to meet annual gross profit targets.
- Analysed sub-product mix relative to product objectives and optimized the effect on profit.
- Conducted pricing studies on competitor's product, resulting in competitive price changes.

1986 to 1989: **SUPERVISOR – INTERNATIONAL**
Supervised order entry, customer service, shipping and documentation, and inside sales functions. Responsible for product training and education of all personnel.

Military: Connecticut National Guard 1985 to present. Rank: Colonel

Given the prominence and bold setting of past positions, no objective or summary statement is needed – assuming Austin wants to stay in a senior sales or marketing position

Searchable terms that make good keywords (shown here in italics)

Key points are bulleted

Notice how earlier positions are given less space

For military no additional info needed – save for interview

Education not required with so much experience unless it adds something new. If used, would go here

The chronological format is the standard. It is easy to prepare and read, follows your history, and is much preferred by recruiters since the screening job goes much faster. However – and this is a big however – what makes it popular with employers is that it makes it easy to screen people *out*. Superficial placement structures driven by the Cog Syndrome favour the candidate who mirrors the job description. Since job descriptions are mostly *activity* focused (based on an existing notion of how the work will be performed) and not *outcome* focused (emphasizing results produced), if your chronology doesn't show the keywords and titles right at the top, you will be headed to the dead letter office before the bigger picture of who you are is seen.

What if you are a spectacular deal maker who works for a non-profit foundation as director of strategic planning, and you want to go back into private industry to bring new insights into international deal-making? The chronological format would not tell the story you want people to read. The functional format would show your capability for managing this kind of work right at the top, so it would get read. Granted, the recruiter would have to do an extra bit of creative thinking.

The same principle applies to the other less conventional formats. Use the chronological format if it works for you, but use the other formats if you have what it takes to do the job well and your last job doesn't reflect that information.

- Do not repeat details common to several positions, unless you need to reinforce some aspect of your skills.

- For each position, include the major results and talents that demonstrate your competency on that job. Secondary results and achievements can be left out if you have been clear about your major accomplishments.

- Always keep your targeted job or work in mind, emphasizing closely related material.

- If you have obtained a formal degree within the past four years, list it at the top of your CV. Otherwise, education should be the last item. *Exception:* if the subject area of your degree is of particular significance to the kind of work you are applying for or you have a relevant advanced degree, keep education at the top of your CV.

- Keep the language clear and crisp. Keep it short.

The Functional CV

The functional CV is organized by functional or skill areas. It is arranged not by date but by the relevance of your strengths to your targeted job. With the functions at the top most obviously supporting the direction you want to go, this format emphasizes your future goals and de-emphasizes your most recent experience. If you're changing jobs or work direction or newly entering or re-entering the job market, the functional format might be the one for you. It also allows you to highlight the skills used in unpaid work experiences such as school, community, or voluntary activities.

The functional format will include abbreviated information about your employment history that will make gaps and unrelated work less obvious. These questions will arise at the interview, or even before, but like a good sales person you have an opportunity this way to get your main message across first.

HOW TO PREPARE A FUNCTIONAL CV

- Use two to four separate functional categories or headings, each one highlighting a particular area of skill or results, such as *Financial Planning, Risk Management, Aggressive Cost Controlling* (see the functions you chose in Part Two, on page 48).

- List your functional categories in order of importance to your targeted job, with the most relevant at the top. The first paragraph should contain the most compelling information. Create different functional CVs for different job targets, each with the functions in a different order.

- Within each functional category, stress the talents and accomplishments that most directly relate to the targeted work. Make a compelling case for your future value.

- List your job history in the last third of the CV, either in order of relevance to the targeted job or chronologically. Show dates, employers, and job titles. If there are gaps to minimize, generalize the dates and offer an explanation in your covering letter or interview.

- List your formal education at the end of your CV, unless you have earned a formal degree within the past four years. If your degree is in a field completely unrelated to your targeted job, list it at the very end, no matter how recently it was received.

- Keep the CV to one page if possible, so the reviewer can see that there is a full chronology at the bottom.

- Pay attention to the covering letter: it directs the reader's attention to your reasons for stressing certain experience.

- Your keyword summary (*Capability Summary* in the example) can be at the top of the CV or the bottom.

Functional Format

In this situation we have an army veteran with fifteen years' service who wants to build on her three years of experience in the restaurant business. She used the **functional** format to keep the emphasis on restaurant management and downplay her fifteen years in the army – mostly in training work – at least until an interview. If she had wished to go back into training, she would have put that category at the top and expanded it considerably, reducing the emphasis on food service

Powerful set of **accomplishments** show both skills and results in the function Restaurant Management

Should consider eliminating reference to being first female manager – not relevant

Chose not to expand on ten years of training work as not the direction she wants to go in now

Reduces attention paid to fifteen years spent in army. Wants to set the stage for discussion about restaurant management first and plans to discuss military experience in interview

CHANTAL MARCOS
244 Arnold Circle
Birmingham, AL 35092
(500) 335-2125
chantmar@yahoo.com

RESTAURANT MANAGEMENT:

- Established total front house system of a 300-seat business. Directed all hiring, training, motivating, and scheduling of 15-person staff. Handled payroll. Managed drink and food orders and all inventory control.

- Interfaced with corporate accounts; successfully building strong relationships and banquet business. Directed unique set-up of three kitchens with three separate menus. Became restaurant's first female manager and handled all operations with equal ease.

- Supervised restaurant makeover from neighbourhood pub to popular bistro-type trendsetter with profitable menu and volume. Dealt with budgets, decorators, building inspectors, hiring, training, menu design, and more.

- Managed army base food service at Fort Leonard Wood. Three facilities responsible for producing over 20,000 meals per week on demanding schedule. Citation for quality control.

INSTRUCTION / TEACHING:

Taught adult classes in organizational strategies, communications skills, team building, and leadership in the US and abroad.

EXPERIENCE:

2000–2003	Houligan's Restaurant & Pub GENERAL MANAGER	Birmingham, AL
1998–2000	Yamiyuri Japanese Restaurant DAY MANAGER	Atlanta, GA
Before 1998	US Army	

EDUCATION: BS UNIVERSITY OF ALABAMA in Food Service Management

CAPABILITY SUMMARY: Budgeting - Scheduling - Food Service Management - Supervising Training - Hiring - Marketing - Facilities Management - Public Relations - Quality Control

Although it is not likely that this candidate will be applying through digital job listing services because her opportunities are local, the **capability** summary at the bottom is a good one and adds a strong list of skills for a potential employer to consider

The Targeted CV

This is the most original CV format you can use. It emphasizes what you can do for an employer by looking at their needs, both immediate and future. The future? Yes, this is the one format that does not limit you to your past. Like an arrow, each version is aimed directly at one job target. It requires sharp focus and is only effective if you pay attention to detail. However, the rewards are well worth the work you put into it. Most career advisers and CV websites don't refer to this format because they haven't seen it in action and because it takes more research work for the applicant to put together. I have used it successfully with job-search clients for years, and have upgraded the approach to be search-engine compatible.

If you are stepping out of the conventional job search – away from 'doing what I have already done' – and know through research that what you can offer to a potential employer is special, this is the format to choose.

Unlike the chronological and functional formats, which emphasize results you have *already* produced, the targeted format emphasizes what you *can* accomplish in the future with a particular company or opportunity – whether you have done it already or not. If you are an architect who has designed quality houses, it's reasonable to believe that you could design and oversee a store project, even if you haven't done so. If you have managed a group of sales people, it would not be difficult for you to convince someone you could manage a group of dealers in the same field. (Of course you would first want to dig into the subject to find out the types of dealer, the special issues, and the relevant terminology.)

HOW TO PREPARE A TARGETED CV

- Use a targeted format when you know exactly what you want. In this format, it is usually necessary to customize each CV for a specific employer or type of position.

- Do your research well. It is required with this format, and it pays big dividends. The more you know about your targeted job or work, the easier it will be to select which capabilities and accomplishments you need to highlight.

- Put a precise Job Target at the top of the CV, right under your name and address. You can name a particular title or describe a function such as *Data Programming Consultant*. Keep it very specific. The test of this target is whether it makes someone working in that field want to read your CV even if they don't have an immediate opening.

  For example: a large car finance company wants to capitalize on its high brand acceptance to launch a number of innovative financial products. The Chief Executive Officer, according to a leading car magazine, has put a priority on this. You have had strong experience in the car industry in fleet sales and customer relations, and you have an MBA in finance. You want to do something new and different. You decide to go for this fresh opportunity.

  You choose as your target *Financial Product Extension* or, more specifically, *Car Financial Product Extension*. You know this will *exclude* most general financial or credit job openings, but in the one area you want to go for, your CV will be read carefully – assuming you get it to the right person. You send it to three people in the company by name: the CEO, the head of product development, and the director of e-commerce. In your covering note, you indicate that you have sent it to all three. You send a copy to the director of HR with the same information.

- Create a first section called *Capabilities*, which is simply a list of short, one- or two-line bulleted statements listing the variety of things you can do to accomplish the aims of your target job. They are in essence a list of '*I can ...*' statements. ('*I can*' is implied, not written.)

  For example, aiming for that car finances job, you would have a list like this:

CAPABILITIES:

- Provide in-depth research in consumer financial products

- Analyse focus group reactions to new products

- Calculate affinity marketing costs

- Provide innovative product leadership

- Develop Internet marketing plans

These are the aspects of the job you think are needed. You know you can do them based on what you have done that is similar. They also serve as a good keyword list and should be written with that in mind.

- Follow the capabilities section with one headed *Accomplishments*. In a bulleted list under this heading, list specific things you have achieved in another job or area that directly or indirectly support your statement of what you know you can do going forwards. It is an *'I have . . .'* listing. These accomplishments or results answer the implied question, 'What have you done in the past to demonstrate that you can do what you say you can in the future?' If you were the architect described earlier, you would list the projects you had designed in the past that were closest to designing a great store. For the above example, you might include such things as:

ACCOMPLISHMENTS:

- Worked closely with car-buying customers on product decisions

- Analysed financial returns on investment opportunities

- Calculated development costs of intangible services

- Designed a customer service website

- Describe your actual work history and education in the bottom third of the CV.

Think about the targeted format this way: every person who has taken on something new that stretched them has had to follow the same process. They had to see what was needed, figure out what they could do about it, and convince someone to give them the chance. It is one of the major weaknesses of the current cog/slot search system that so much relies on past experience. It works against cross-fertilization. If you use a targeted format, you look freshly at things, and those companies that encourage change will be most interested.

Targeted CV

In this type of CV a very clear Job Target must be used so it goes right to the attention of the reader

E-mail is a valuable communications asset – show it

This entire list of capabilities consists of results Madison is confident he can achieve. To be capable is to be able to do, not to have done. Analyse the job first, then define what you can do to make it happen

Keeping in mind what he has said he can do, Madison now wants to present the closest match of things he has already accomplished to support his claims

This CV format is not about past history, but the employment history is obviously relevant in this case. In many others, the target is in a direction that diverges from the past

ELLIOT R. MADISON
1222 Hickory Drive Seville, CO 81009
Phone (303) 555-5424
erm12@att.net

JOB TARGET   Automotive Financial Product Line Extension

CAPABILITIES
Provide in-depth research in consumer financial products
Analyse focus group reactions to new products
Calculate affinity marketing costs
Make forecasts and define metrics
Produce detailed competitive market scans
Design effective test marketing

ACCOMPLISHMENTS
Designed successful new product launches
Performed market research and assessments
Calculated development costs of intangibles
Worked closely with automotive dealers and customers
Managed third-party accessories business
Served on product-design team
Managed e-commerce business

WORK HISTORY 1991 – present
AUTO BY TEL: Seville, Col. Marketing Coordinator
KB MARKETS: Ann Arbor, Mich. Market Researcher
CAR STOP SERVICES: Ann Arbor, Mich. Financial Analyst

EDUCATION
1990 UNIVERSITY OF MICHIGAN BS Accounting
Subject: Consumer Credit

The CV Alternative Format

How do multi-faceted, talented men and women who have a history of non-traditional work experiences but want to join the more conventional workforce express themselves in the two-dimensional search engine environment?

The answer is not easily. The process of fitting varied life, work, and learning experiences into a mechanized 'fill the slots' search system is daunting and could well be a waste of time. On the other hand, when talented people with rich and unconventional lives (an author, an ex-athlete, a community activist, a woman who took ten years off to educate her three children at home) succumb to just networking and 'looking around', they all too often end up in work below their capabilities that pays next to nothing – because there are no categories they easily fit into. Employment agencies don't have the energy to try, company employment offices get puzzled, and nothing fits in the digital machinery.

If you are in the non-traditional category, the first principle is this: go after the kind of job that will offer you the opportunity to continue your fulfilling life and that will provide great results for your employer. Do not settle for conformity if it means slowing down the passion and meaning of your life. Slowing down the pace is OK; tossing away your spirit is not. If you do not use a conventional CV, you will have a more difficult time getting all the interviews you want, but when you do find your next occupation, your skills and accomplishments will shine through and propel you forwards.

The CV alternative letter is the way to reach employers if the other formats don't work for you. It is a customized letter to a person who can make or influence employment decisions, in which you communicate your strengths in a way that lets them see how to put you to good use in their organization. It is a substitute for a CV, and gives you more flexibility in choosing opportunities and expressing your talents. Like the targeted CV, you vary the letter for each opportunity that you pursue.

A CV alternative fits a number of needs:

- A person who didn't get the degree that is required can show a level of results that exceeds that of other applicants.

- A person with gaps in job continuity that could knock them out of consideration can use the letter to explain or justify those gaps.

- A person who has none of the skills listed in the job requirement can demonstrate that they know how to accomplish the same or better results another way.

- A person transferring from one field to another where it appears on the surface that their past job skills are not relevant will be able to make connections that the firm might not have seen otherwise.

- A person with a disability or other special circumstances can explain it in a way that removes any blocks for the position.

Here's what the CV alternative letter communicates:

- The specific outcomes or results you can produce for the organization.

- Why you are putting this in letter format rather than in a conventional CV.

- How the person reading the letter can find out more about you and feel confident about what you have presented.

HOW TO PREPARE A CV ALTERNATIVE LETTER

- Do enough research to learn about the company and ensure you know its size and scope, its competitors, its customer needs, its markets and products, and its financial condition. Also find out what you can about the industry itself.

- Find out what you can do for one or more divisions or functions of the company, how your particular talents fit in better than more conventional hiring solutions. Back that up with specific information about your competencies and experience – go beyond '*I think I can help you in this . . .*'

- Know the person to whom you are sending the letter by name, position, and if possible reputation in the field, or by referral from another person.

- Keep the letter to one page.

- Suggest what the next steps should be.

- Have someone knowledgeable in the field review the letter and proofread it.

- Send it two ways – by e-mail (as an attachment if they take attachments) and by first-class post.

- Prepare. Act as if the employer is going to call you the next day, and know how to back up what you said you could accomplish. Make a list of specific answers to anticipated questions, as well as personal references.

- Follow up with a phone call to the person within three days of when you expect them to have received the letter.

- If during the follow-up you are requested to send a CV, send a copy of the letter along with it for reference. (Consider using the functional or targeted formats.)

CV Alternative Document

Having attractive letterhead stationery is essential for looking professional

E-mail is a must for business contacting

JOAN PEERZY
1756 COLORADO DRIVE
PASADENA, CA 12345
555 123 4567
peerzy@internetprovider.com

17 March, 2003
Mrs. Solon Hendricks CEO
Acusel, Inc
443 Rosefair Dr.
Pasadena, CA 12345

Dear Mrs. Hendricks,

Reference to a recent event is a great opening, as is naming a mutual professional contact

Congratulations on your recent award as one of the most innovative new companies in Southern California. Everyone who has followed your growth is delighted to hear of your recognition and what went behind it. Miles Fortune, with whom I serve on the Pasadena Employment Training Team, has told me a lot about your business, and how you have grown from three people to over two dozen.

Right up front acknowledges that there is a reason for not sending a conventional CV. No apology needed

I am sending this letter in lieu of a CV since I don't believe a conventional CV would give a clear picture of what I think I can offer your firm.

I am an excellent interviewer and 'talent scout' and will be able to help you staff top talent for your future growth. At Pasadena Community College I was a feature writer and interviewed dozens of people for articles. I know how to ask tough questions without offence, and to write up what I find accurately. On the PETT project I interviewed volunteers and assigned them to appropriate work. In this same programme I became very familiar with all the local colleges and training programmes and built good relations with the placement offices.

Talks specifically about the kind of value she can offer and how she is certain of this

Shows she has done her research and is not doing a circular letter – states her needs clearly

A good interviewer needs to understand a variety of non-discrimination practices and protocols, and I have just finished researching these requirements on the state website. I am in touch with a member of our local Personnel Resources Association branch and he has checked my knowledge and found it to be up to date. He has also familiarized me with a number of contemporary assessment resources. Based on what I know about Acusel, I am assuming you do not yet have a full-time Personnel Manager or Recruiter. If this is true, I would like to apply for the position. I can be flexible about my hours in the first months, but will want to work a minimum of 25 hours per week and expand as your needs grow, as I am sure they will.

When would be a good time for us to meet and discuss how I can contribute to your continued success? My schedule next week is flexible. I'll phone you soon.

Politely yet firmly shows her intention of meeting

Sincerely,

Joan Peerzy

CV Do's and Don'ts

Read each of the paragraphs below and check your understanding of the principles we are espousing for your perfect CV. Circle the mark in front of the paragraph to indicate those you are ready to follow for yourself.

CV DO'S

- To get the most mileage out of your CV, always prepare it with one or more targeted jobs or assignments in mind (a different CV for each), and state this in your objective statement. This will help you determine what to include or leave out.

- When listing accomplishments or duties, use short, indented, easy-to-read (bulleted) phrases. Change these to dashes (—) or asterisks (*) when converting to digital form.

- Choose the clearest, simplest language to say what you want to say, while still including the necessary keywords for database retrieval.

- Emphasize outcomes, not activities. To say, *Was responsible for training our customer service reps* (activity orientation) is less powerful than saying, *My training of customer service reps increased documented customer satisfaction by 50 per cent.*

- Use specific quantities, percentages, or monetary values where they enhance your description of a result.

- Put the strongest statements at the top of each section or paragraph. Keep in mind that what can be seen on the monitor without scrolling – equivalent to 'above the fold' in a newspaper – is most likely to get read.

- Include any military experience with your rank. If you have had a full military career, treat it just like work experience – explaining any esoteric experience or skills in lay terms.

- Include community and voluntary work if it shows something about you that you want the employer to know, or if it covers employment time gaps.

- Choose the font style and size carefully. What looks good on a printed document may not look good on a computer screen. Times, Helvetica, and Arial work well in either form. For digital use, we prefer 14-point type for screen readability; however, if you use 12-point, you will get more information on each screen. Don't use 10-point or smaller type except for references to articles, publications, or other documents.

- Have someone with good language skills and familiarity with your profession check for appropriate wording, spelling, punctuation, and grammar.

- Make sure all keywords and phrases relevant to your target field are listed as statements and accomplishments and are as close to the top as possible.

- State what you have accomplished in the most powerful and compelling terms. Don't be afraid of bragging; on the other hand, don't hype the description; make it 'we accomplished…'.

- Make your objective statement meaningful and relevant to the work you are applying for. Avoid generalities.

- If you have published professional articles and other materials, mention them briefly. Provide additional information when requested. Mention professional affiliations if they are relevant.

- If you are willing to relocate, say so in the covering letter.

CV DON'TS

- Don't list references or say they are 'available upon request'. This is implied.

- Don't enclose your CV in a binder or folder.

- Don't include information about your gender, age, height and weight, race, religion, state of health, or other personal or family data.

- Don't include a photograph.

- Don't include the postal address of previous employers. County (or country if you have worked outside Britain) is sufficient.

- Don't include salary information. This will be negotiated separately. If requested by an employer, include it in the covering letter.

- Limit the use of the personal pronoun *I*. It is implied throughout.

- Don't use Greek, Latin, scientific terms, or foreign languages unless you know in advance that the organization's tracking and screening software can handle it.

- Don't include hobbies or social interests unless they clearly contribute to your ability to perform the targeted job or assignment.

- Don't fax your CV unless you are specifically requested to do so.

- Avoid gratuitous self-descriptions, such as *seasoned self-starter*.

- Don't discuss your reasons for leaving your previous position – save it for the interview unless it is crucial to explain a gap or change (i.e., left to pursue my master's degree full time).

7

The Importance of Custom Tailoring

One size does not fit all when it comes to CVs. At the moment, the system is so employer- and vendor-controlled that it takes special astuteness to go around or get through the narrow slots and filters of the digital gateway and achieve the person-to-person contact that will significantly improve your chances of meeting the right people face to face.

One key to success is tailoring each CV approach to each type of job target or, in some cases, to the needs of a specific employer.

Consider this question: if a candidate with approximately the same skills as you sent a standardized CV to twenty-five employers and you sent a customized letter and CV addressing the specific needs of each of just ten of those employers, who would get the most interviews? The customized approach will work better every time. Think about it: a basic premise of almost all contemporary marketing is that the more you can customize your product to the user's needs, the higher your sales will be, everything else being equal. I've tracked users of outplacement and CV programs and found that customization makes the CV several times more successful. Of course there are degrees of customization and pay-off, some requiring more research than others. How much effort to put into customizing is an important decision you need to make as you translate your Job Targets and talent into compelling requests for interviews with the people who can offer you what you want.

One CV Does Not Fit All

People have various skills and talents – some complementary, some independent, some unique, some commonplace. Most job searchers can combine their skills and talents in a number of ways. If you have a battery of skills and experiences, it's hard to put together one CV that includes everything. You will want to design different CVs for different job directions. Some will play up your talent in certain areas; others will highlight different strengths.

If this is your situation, prepare a number of CV paragraphs and phrases. Copy and store them in lists or as files in a digital folder so you can pull different paragraphs for different submissions. New skills and results can be added to your database as they're attained.

Commercial CV preparation services do little to customize your CVs beyond one general target. Digital job-search services can't do it. Private recruiters or executive search services will help prepare your CV for a particular job they are interested in filling. However, you are the main player in achieving success in the CV game. Since fewer than 10 per cent of all CVs are customized to address the needs of the company to which they are sent, every step you take to focus your CV on the needs and situations of specific employers brings you more (and better) job offers.

You Are Not Your Job Title

If you are a seasoned employee, you have accumulated years of experience, competencies, skills, education, accomplishments, relationships, and work styles. There are many things you have done, and can do. You can fit into a variety of situations and adapt to many challenges. You have probably already had a variety of occupations.

How do you avoid being typecast into slots that represent old job titles or past competencies? It's difficult, because superficial thinking, aided and abetted by digital job-search engines, is programmed to find people who have already done what's intrinsic to the current job description. Mass-market job titles – what we called the Cog Syndrome (see page 17) – work that way. If you are already a research librarian, you will be spindled, stapled, and sorted into only the 'research librarian' slots in the electronic galaxy of search engines. If company libraries haven't converted to a brand-new process called, say, 'multiple-factor cross-functional search procedures', that idea won't be in their job descriptions. If you have experience in this and it would be a valuable addition to the company, perhaps you'll be the one to introduce it – but you'll have to go outside the conventional search filters to get them to recognize it.

Customize What?

When you have identified a specific company and gone beyond their basic job listings to gain some 'insider knowledge' about the organization, you will want to customize the CV and covering message or letter to point out how you will be a very good fit for that company.

Your CV can be customized to enhance the effectiveness and focus of your job search. Here are three areas:

Customized target Decide in advance which two or three target jobs you are after so you can focus each CV differently. For example, *Editor, Researcher, Writer* involve work in a common field and use related skills, yet each requires a different CV focus to put that talent in the top position.

Customized format Based on your current situation – your recent work history, the relevance of past work to present targets, your need for part- or full-time work, returning to work after an absence, moving from freelance to salaried or vice versa – you will want to choose the right format to use from the ones described in the last chapter. Each has its own advantages and disadvantages.

Customized delivery You can also customize your delivery options based on the employer's needs. You will probably use CVs that are both digital (Internet) and presentation (sent through the post or taken to an interview). It is generally best to start with the presentation form and then convert to digital form when you need to. Most examples in this book are shown in presentation form.

8

Write Like a Reporter

When you have a job interview, you dress well to make the best impression. *Dress for Success* is not only a bestselling book, but also fundamental to good job-hunting. When you prepare your CV, there is an equivalent process: *Write Like a Reporter*. The story you want to tell will only get read if your writing grabs the prospective employer's attention.

First and Last Basic Rules

A bit about the risks: a major job-placement firm in the US recently reported that according to its studies, between 15 per cent and 20 per cent of the job searchers who passed through the various gateways to reach a live reader lost their opportunity to be considered because of basic errors in their CVs: misspellings, bad grammar, poor organization of information, lack of responsiveness to what the company was looking for, not putting the most important stuff up front, using five pages to communicate two pages' worth of information, complaining about their old employer.

Basic rule: 'double edit' any CV – digital or presentation – before you send it to recruiters. Someone with knowledge of the field and a good business sense should do the first edit. Someone who has sound writing skills should do the second edit. Even experienced writers need and want editing of their work. It's strength, not weakness, to turn to an editor for a review. It's the kind of quality control any professional would use on the job.

Lead with the Best Points

Good reporters make certain that their first paragraphs compel you to read further. The same common-sense principle applies to CVs. After your contact information, the next thing the reader sees should be something that makes them say *Yes!* and read on with heightened interest.

If you are a recent graduate, listing your degree (and specialization if it relates) at the top is fine. If you are using a chronological CV, the name of your most recent employer and your title should relate to the company's needs and will show at the top. If your most recent employer is in a totally different field and your last job title is different from the job you want, consider changing the format.

If you put an objective at the top of the CV, then you are right on target *if* your objective speaks directly to what the employer is seeking. If it is totally different – they are looking for a researcher and your objective is to find a place in marketing and sales – a recruiter might be tempted to turn to the next CV. An overly general objective will probably get by – *A solid organization that offers an opportunity to learn and grow* – but you gain nothing. You've wasted a headline and an opportunity. Many objective statements are either so broad that they add nothing or so narrow that they don't fit the company's needs. Fortunately, most good recruiters know that a very specific objective not in line with what they want is not a reason to pass on an otherwise good CV.

Before writing your CV, review your Selling Case (see page 43) – the summary statement that shows your unique value to a particular enterprise. Interweave that into both your CV and covering letter. A Selling Case would be something like:

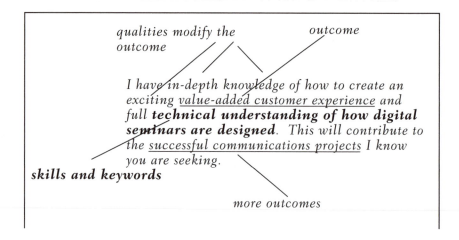

qualities modify the outcome

outcome

I have in-depth knowledge of how to create an exciting *value-added customer experience* and full **technical understanding of how digital seminars are designed**. This will contribute to the *successful communications projects* I know you are seeking.

skills and keywords

more outcomes

What a good reporter and a good CV writer are after is for the reader to settle back thinking, *This is interesting* ... and then read further with special attention. Unless you have really captured the recruiter's attention – as a well-done targeted CV can do, since it has the employer's needs in mind – they will probably give it only a mechanical screening.

Organize the Layout

To ensure readability, a newspaper reporter wants to see that the headlines and subheads are in the right order, that the piece is easy to read, and that the facts are there.

The average CV will get less than two minutes of attention on the first scan, so the need for having a good layout is obvious. People don't necessarily read your CV from top to bottom, so your layout should make it easy for readers to find what they are seeking. Your critical sales points should be obvious.

Writing Style

Shorter is better. Compare this statement:

I was responsible for interfacing with the department that gathered the customer information from the dealers, and then put it into the right format for the offices to read.

with:

> Converted customer data into executive presentations.

Or compare this:

> I used the computer to convert two-dimensional drawings to
> 3-D elevations that we showed to clients for feedback.

with:

> Highly qualified using CAD equipment to prepare client
> presentations.

Good reporters, and good CV writers, use the minimum number of words necessary to convey an idea with punch.

In preparing your CV, pay attention to how different terms are used:

> When describing an **action** – from a job duty or function – use
> an active verb at the start of the sentence: *converted . . .,*
> *translated . . ., developed. . . .* You will find a list of active verbs
> on page 46.

> When describing a **skill,** preface it with a qualifier, such as
> *experienced* web master or *master* carpenter.

> When communicating an **accomplishment**, define the
> tangible results, not just the activity. Quantify results when
> you can: *Managed Sales Centre, achieving 20 per cent*
> *improvement in customer satisfaction in three months.*

Since most CVs are subject to scanning and tracking systems, specify your skills as accurately as possible and use them in different phrases. *Risk management* is the skill, *Risk Manager* is the job title. Since you do not know in advance how the company might be scanning or searching, you should use both.

Objective, Opening Paragraph, and Keyword List

A concise *opening paragraph* description of your skills – your Selling Case, perhaps – aimed at the recipient of your CV will prompt interest. This paragraph is longer and more detailed than the one- or two-line *objective statement* that precedes it. You could say that the objective statement 'positions' the CV, and the opening paragraph makes a case for the writer's qualifications. Here is an example:

Objective: Web Page Designer

> OPENING PARAGRAPH
> My experience with a variety of web design languages, combined with expertise using FrontPage, Dreamweaver, and other graphic applications, plus a master's degree in Communication Arts, makes me a skilled producer of productive websites for business units.

A *summary of qualifications* is a five- or six-line keyword list that quickly fleshes out the scope of your skills to those who read your CV. It can be used in place of the opening paragraph, and it can be customized for each kind of position you go for. In the example below, the writer broadened his appeal beyond web page designer. Using the summary of qualifications rather than the opening paragraph can allow more flexibility in the objective statement, and in the covering letter.

> SUMMARY OF QUALIFICATIONS
> Teach business-writing skills to employees
> Edit web pages for brevity and relevance
> Maintain interesting content in press releases
> Ensure that training materials are accurate and well written
> Prepare internal information releases

Layout, Typing, and Typography for Presentation CVs

The presentation CV is the one that will show up best in print. Its emphasis is on visual organization of data, and the time you spend getting this right is not wasted. You will need a printed version of your presentation CV for every face-to-face encounter you have. Once your presentation CVs are ready, you can convert them to digital form where needed. Having both styles available gives you the best chance in the interview and in passing your CV to others for networking.

Elements that contribute to a good presentation CV layout include:

- UPPERCASE LETTERS, used for important headings or titles only.

- Bulleted and indented text for short statements of qualification.

- *Italics* and **bold,** used sparingly to highlight key terms you want to take the reader's eye to. (Bold and italic type will be eliminated when you convert to digital.)

- Use headings for the main three to five divisions, but do not use headings entitled 'CV', 'Name', or 'Address', as these are obvious.

- Use underlining rarely except for web links.

- Create an airy look in your CV with wide margins, careful positioning of your name and address, spacing between paragraphs, and indentations. Good print advertising makes generous use of empty space on the page. It helps to accent what is on the page in a way that is restful to the eye and mind.

- Make sure your name, address, phone number, and e-mail address are flush left or centred at the top of your CV. If you do not want to be called at work, do not include your work or mobile phone numbers. If you are away at college, show both a 'permanent' phone number and address and your current information.

- Use one-inch margins on all sides of the page.

- Single-space the text of your CV. Double-space between paragraphs.

Do Several Drafts

Don't expect to achieve a finished CV with your first draft. Plan to revise several times for each format you use. Once you have assembled all your pertinent data, edit it carefully, cutting back sentences that are too long and eliminating repetitions and unclear language. Use the double-edit process suggested at the beginning of this topic. You want your final version to be a highly polished product. This investment will pay off for you.

CHECKLIST FOR FINAL REVIEW

- The material fits neatly on one or two pages.

- There are no spelling, grammar, or punctuation errors.

- Your name, address, phone number, and e-mail address are centred or flush left at the top.

- Paragraphs and section lengths are appropriate to their importance.

- Keywords relative to your job target are included and checked against company needs.

- Bold or capital letters are used to emphasize important titles, but not to excess.

- Indentations are used to separate different areas and organize information logically.

- Extraneous personal information (height, weight, age, gender, hobbies) has been excluded.

- Sentences and paragraphs are edited to eliminate unnecessary or repetitious information.

- The printed page is neat, clean, and professional looking.

9

Digital vs. Presentation CVs

More Facts of Life in the Digital Age

Today, there is some good – and a lot of bad – digital CV news. The good news is that if you have done a superb job of researching your job targets and have compiled a list of keyword skills and competencies that are highly relevant to the job description, a company looking for those exact skills will quickly find you. This is a big advantage for those whose skills are easily definable, very specific, and highly recognizable.

The bad news is that if you don't get the relevant language right or get too abstract or use a generalized 'one-size-fits-all' approach, the electronic filing systems that hold your CV among millions of others may never discover you. Most medium to large companies prefer electronic CVs because they are easier to track in their applicant tracking systems. This doesn't mean that they are best for you, but you must know how to master them.

Digital or otherwise, a CV scores readership by having the right keywords, statements, and phrases. Even in the days when CVs were only reviewed by the human eye, it was the same. If your CV was full of wind-up phrases, superfluous information, or repetition, the reader's eyes glazed over, and in a minute or two it went into the Reject for

Now pile or was sent to CV Siberia to languish in files that were periodically dumped.

Any document created using a word-processing software program is in a sense digital. However, this is not the popular understanding of what a digital CV is. A digital CV is one that is *delivered* digitally or *converted* to ASCII or plain text format after delivery.

A presentation CV is designed, formatted, and printed for the human eye to review. You will undoubtedly be using a word processor to compose your presentation CV. Right from your first contact with your targeted employer, that CV must look good, effectively present your skills and accomplishments, and be correctly formatted, critiqued, edited, and printed.

A digital CV is one that has been designed initially, or converted from your presentation CV, to be most effectively used on the Internet or with electronic search or sorting programs designed to transmit documents by common computer messaging protocols – normally ASCII or plain text. The main difference between the two types of CV is that one is meant to be processed by a human reader and the other by a computer search engine: a human can assess a variety of combinations of format, layout, language, and writing styles, and interpret the relationships. The computer systems in use today can only recognize discrete words and phrases that match other words and phrases; they can't interpret formats, infer hierarchies, recognize type styles like bold or italic; interpret the meanings of sentences or paragraphs, or make comparisons that mean much.

The digitizing process starts by shredding your well-designed presentation CV into definable slugs and symbols. Then the file can be updated, sent to subsidiaries or related recruiters, folded, squeezed, analysed, e-mailed, and used in so many ways that you will want to read the privacy policy terms of any company you send it to – especially commercial job-search services. Talk about broadcasting your identity! Here is your past, your economic worth, your postal address, phone number, and e-mail address, and your entire work history, spread out all over the place. And, of course, it can be reassembled again whenever desired – which could turn out to be just what you want if the job of your dreams comes up.

Computer search engines are great at finding selected keywords and phrases in a million documents in a few seconds, but then the interpretation of the relationships between them has to be done by a human. Unfortunately for the humans, if the computer doesn't find a CV matching the search terms, the human won't even get to see it.

Your CV will be delivered through the post, by hand, or electronically to a company you've researched well. What happens then? When it's sent through the post, especially in medium to large companies, and if you haven't addressed it to a specific person, a personnel clerk may unceremoniously feed it into a digital scanner. If it is a pre-formatted electronic CV, a recruiter or clerk, or automatic e-mail address, will put it into a presorting program. The presorting program directs your data through a set of search-engine nomenclature filters that separate out CVs with terms for jobs that someone in the company is filling now. If you're lucky, you make the hallowed 'shortlist', and you will probably get a phone call or e-mail asking further questions. If you don't survive the first pass, your CV goes to a vast storage farm with thousands of other CVs for the company to peruse at its own pace, using search categories and terminology it alone controls.

If you are staying with a broad and generalized approach instead of customizing your CV for each submission as we recommend, do the digital conversion yourself. This allows you to accomplish basic formatting in advance, which makes the best of the limited choices available.

Below are several ways you can enter your CV into the digital machinery. (One major caveat: many smaller companies, specialized fields, and big companies seeking top executive and professional employees have not yet embraced digitizing, and neither have many government offices. However, the digitizing trend is quickly catching on in those places, too. Check first.)

Types of Digital CV

Attachment CVs are those that are designed and laid out as presentation CVs using a common word-processing program – usually Microsoft Word – and included as an 'attachment' to an e-mail message. The reader reviews the covering letter message in the e-mail and decides whether to download the attachment and open it. From here the reader can read it, print it out, or, having reviewed it, send it along to be digitized for future retrieval. Your best bet is to use the attachment CV approach where you can because the recipient can see the full layout and read it the way you want. Unfortunately, because of viruses, mailbox limitations, and other constraints, some companies won't want to receive attachments from outside their firewalls.

E-mail CVs are embedded into the body of an e-mail message, usually as requested in an advertised listing (online or printed) or in response to a specific request from an employer. These CVs are usually sent to an e-mail address that automatically scans them into a database. Before you send a CV by e-mail, remember that it will lose a lot of its formatting – italics, bold, indentations, and so on. Try it out by e-mailing it to yourself first, and then making formatting adjustments until you get the look you want. Then send it out.

Scannable CVs are printed CVs that are sent by regular post or delivered by hand to a firm and then fed into an optical scanner that converts them into digital CVs. The paper copy is usually thrown away. Scanning is a practice that is on its way out because of the shortcomings of character recognition software.

Job bank or CV distribution services accept either a 'profile', where the service asks you to fill in a form highlighting contact information and key skills, job titles, degrees, and so on, or a 'paste-in' CV. The profiles tend to look like linear versions of old-fashioned application forms, with no room for accomplishments or such items as personal qualities. The alternative is a space where you can cut and paste your CV into the site. Here is where you will want to be careful. Don't simply paste your presentation form CV into the box because it will be automatically converted to ASCII or plain text, and all the formatting, tabs, indents, bullets, bold text, underlining, type fonts, and headings will be gone. It is far better to do your own conversion to ASCII beforehand using the limited yet useful formatting you can still do in this style. See the process below.

The Challenge of Digital

Your presentation CV is the one you print on good-quality paper and take with you to interviews. You design it to create a visual impact as well as to convey information. Often, it is also what you send as an attachment by e-mail. If the employer or recruiter who receives it has the same word-processing program as you (such as Word, WordPerfect, or AppleWorks), they can open the file on their computer, download or print it, and your CV will be just as you designed it.

However – and this is a big however – if your CV is not received first by a person who wants to read it (your covering letter will have a lot to do with this), it will probably be forwarded to a company site that automatically converts it into digital format for later search and retrieval. When your CV hits those digital conversions, your careful formatting will be lost, replaced by what is known as ASCII/plain text. This is the standard computer text format that is used by all search engines and computer databases worldwide.

ASCII stands for American Standard Code of Information Interchange. It uses a character set that can be interpreted by virtually every operating system. This compatibility is achieved by eliminating distinctive software instructions for such elements as font size, font style, and tab spacing. It is the formatting used in most e-mail worldwide.

Basically, your CV goes from this: to this:

Sarah Featherstone
featherstone@internetprovider.com

Campus: Permanent:
555-123-4567 (cell)   555-321-5674

OBJECTIVE: Public Accounting Auditor In The Greater Pittsburgh Area

SUMMARY:
- Two years of progressive accounting and auditing
- Auditor internship with Deloitte and Touche in New York City
- Proficient with MS Office, Windows XP, and the Internet

EXPERIENCE:
Auditor Trainee, May 2003 to August 2003
Deloitte and Touche, New York, NY
- Participated in the annual audit of Carrigan Holdings, including development of the final certification report.
- Participated in quarterly audit of Solomon Bank Corporation, including identification and correction of over thirty major accounting errors.

Accounts Payable/Bookkeeping Clerk, May 2003 to August 2003
Gainesville Tax and Bookkeeping Service, Gainesville, FL
- Assisted (via remote) with payroll, tax, and account processing. Developed automated monthly sales tax payment system.
- Implemented Rapid Tax Refund service for individual customers.

EDUCATION:
Bachelor of Business Administration in Accounting, Expected May 2004
University of Philadelphia, Philadelphia, PA

Managerial Accounting   Corporate Audit and Reconciliation
Intermediate Accounting I & II   Financial Management
Accounting I & II   Internal Audit

Sarah Featherstone
featherstone@internetprovider.com
Campus: 555-123-4567 (cell)
Permanent: 555-321-5674
OBJECTIVE: Public Accounting Auditor In The Greater Pittsburgh Area
SUMMARY:
Two years of progressive accounting and auditing
Auditor internship with Deloitte and Touche in New York City
Proficient with MS Office, Windows XP, and the Internet
EXPERIENCE:
Auditor Trainee, May 2003 to August 2003
Deloitte and Touche, New York, NY
Participated in the annual audit of Carrigan Holdings, including development of the final certification report.
Participated in quarterly audit of Solomon Bank Corporation, including identification and correction of over thirty major accounting errors.
Accounts Payable/Bookkeeping Clerk, May 2003 to August 2003
Gainesville Tax and Bookkeeping Service, Gainesville, FL
Assisted (via remote) with payroll, tax, and account processing. Developed automated monthly sales tax payment system.
Implemented Rapid Tax Refund service for individual customers.
EDUCATION:
Bachelor of Business Administration in Accounting, Expected May 2004
University of Philadelphia, Philadelphia, PA
Managerial Accounting Corporate Audit and Reconciliation
Intermediate Accounting I & II Financial Management
Accounting I & II Internal Audit

When you know your CV will be converted to digital form, it is best to convert a version of your presentation CV to ASCII in advance so you can at least achieve the best that this format allows. Once you've done that, it will be easy to send your ASCII CV in the body of an e-mail – in addition to an attachment version – thus allowing the presentation version to be read and the ASCII version to be stored. You'll also be able to easily cut and paste the preformatted ASCII version into online CV databases or corporate recruiting sites. You can send both a presentation CV and a digital CV to the same person, one for reading and one for the digital files.

On the following two pages you will see why a good reformatting is worth the time it takes, once you have converted to ASCII/plain text.

Presentation CV in Microsoft Word
before conversion to plain text

Janann Bethany Howard
7877 Morrissey Avenue
Pleasantville, NY 12345
(555) 123-4567
howard@internetprovider.com

OBJECTIVE: **Software Sales Management**

2002–present   STOCKWOOD COMMUNICATIONS, Yonkers, NY
Programme Manager
- Manage a customer service/marketing programme targeting the company's top customers nationally, resulting in $775K sales/year.
- Identify opportunities, formulate strategies, and implement plans to stimulate sales of company's microcomputer software product line.
- Supervise staff of six; develop and promote internal talent.

1995-2002   CORLEY HEALTH ASSOCIATES, Bend, OR
Senior Administrator
- Developed decision papers for trustees and executives of $360 million budget HMO.
- Identified organizational impact of issues and recommended alternative options.
- Edited managerial materials for presentation to board, consulting senior-level executives in developing information.
Assistant Office Director
- Supervised staff of six.
- Oversaw transition of office to fully automated office system, resulting in increased staff productivity and higher morale. Wrote newsletters and speeches for trustees.
- Developed and refined a computerized database management program, improving speed in retrieving information used in decision making.
- Managed a reduction in staff due to organizational budget cuts, maintaining productivity standard with fewer staff members.

1990-1995   AMERICAN ASSOCIATION OF RETIRED PERSONS, Washington, DC
Legislative Specialist
- Researched, analysed, and reported legislative interests of association's membership.
- Organized association's first formal legislative correspondence section, improving response time to over 1,500 letters received each month.

EDUCATION

1995   UNIVERSITY OF WASHINGTON, Seattle, WA
Master of Public Administration
ELMIRA COLLEGE, Elmira, NY
BA Political Science, cum laude

Presentation CV on page 101
converted to plain text and reformatted

With ALL CAPS used for emphasis, page returns adjusted to break up text into blocks, asterisks substituted for bulleted text, and line breaks adjusted, the original ASCII conversion has been made to look more organized with emphasis where needed.

Janann Bethany Howard
7877 Morrissey Avenue
Pleasantville, NY 12345
(555) 123-4567
howard@internetprovider.com

OBJECTIVE: SOFTWARE SALES MANAGEMENT

EXPERIENCE:
2002–present
STOCKWOOD COMMUNICATIONS, Yonkers, NY
PROGRAMME MANAGER
* Manage a customer service/marketing programme targeting the company's top
  customers nationally, resulting in $775K sales/year.
* Identify opportunities, formulate strategies, and implement plans to stimulate sales
  of company's microcomputer software product line.
* Supervise staff of six; develop and promote internal talent.

1995-2002
CORLEY HEALTH ASSOCIATES, Bend, OR
SENIOR ADMINISTRATOR
* Developed decision papers for trustees and executives of $360 million budget HMO.
* Identified organizational impact of issues and recommended alternative options.
* Edited managerial materials for presentation to board, consulting senior-level
  executives in developing information.

ASSISTANT OFFICE DIRECTOR
* Supervised staff of six.
* Oversaw transition of office to fully automated office system, resulting in increased staff
  productivity and higher morale. Wrote newsletters and speeches for trustees.
* Developed and refined a computerized database management program, improving
  speed in retrieving information used in decision-making.
* Managed a reduction in staff due to organizational budget cuts, maintaining
  productivity standards with fewer staff members.

1990-1995
AMERICAN ASSOCIATION OF RETIRED PERSONS, Washington, DC
LEGISLATIVE SPECIALIST
* Researched, analysed, and reported legislative interests of association's membership.
* Organized association's first formal legislative correspondence section, improving
  response time to over 1,500 letters received each month.

EDUCATION
1995
UNIVERSITY OF WASHINGTON, Seattle, WA
Master of Public Administration

ELMIRA COLLEGE: Elmira, NY
BA Political Science, cum laude

How to Change Presentation CVs into ASCII CVs

It is best to create two ASCII CVs on your computer: the first to paste into the body of e-mails and the second to paste into online forms at job-search or company websites. The procedure is slightly different for each. (These instructions are for Microsoft Word, the word-processing program used by two-thirds of the market. Similar steps are used in other word-processing programs.)

FOR E-MAILS:

1. Open your presentation CV.

2. Save the file, using a different file name.

   - Click *File*, then *Save as*. In the box that appears, next to *File name*, type in the name of your file followed by *e* for e-mail and add a number if you will have several digital CVs. It is also helpful to insert the word *digital* into the file name. End with *.txt* (for example, *my CV.doc* becomes *my_digital_CV_e1.txt*).

   - In that same dialogue box, where you see *Save as type*, select *Text only* **with line breaks**.

   - Click *Save*.

3. Paste the file into an e-mail.

   - Launch Notepad (for PCs, or TextEdit for Macs) by clicking the *Start* button on your lower tool bar, then clicking *Programs*, then *Accessories*, then *Notepad*.

   - Open the text file (*my_digital_CV_e1.txt*). You can now set spacing and line breaks, change some words to all caps, add dashes or asterisks, and make a few other adjustments to clean up your digital CV.

   - Click *Edit*, then *Select all*.

   - Right-click your mouse and select *Copy*.

   - Launch your e-mail program and start a new e-mail.

   - With the cursor blinking in the body of the e-mail message, right-click your mouse and select *Paste*.

- Address the e-mail. Fill in the subject line. If you are applying for an advertised position, refer to it by name and number in that line. In the body of the e-mail, add a covering note or letter ahead of the CV. Click *Send*.

   Tip: To see how the CV will look when delivered, first send the file to yourself and perhaps to a friend with a different e-mail program.

   Tip: If you are really knowledgeable about e-mail and want to make your CV look even better, and if you know the type of e-mail application that the recipient uses, change the text wrap settings in your e-mail application to the same settings, or use a fail-safe lower setting of sixty to seventy characters. This will make for better line breaks when it is received on the other end.

FOR INPUTTING TO ONLINE PROFILES:

1. Open your presentation CV.

2. Save the file, using a different file name.

- Click *File,* then *Save as.* In the box that appears, next to *File name,* type in the name of your file, with *digital* inserted, followed by *o* for online. Add a number to identify which CV you are using. End with *.txt* (for example, *my_CV.doc* becomes *my_digital_CV_o1.txt*).

- In that same box, where you see *Save as type,* select *Text only* or *Text only **without line breaks***.

- Launch Notepad by clicking the *Start* button on your lower tool bar, then clicking *Programs,* then *Accessories,* then *Notepad.* Or use TextEdit in Mac.

- Open the text file (*my_digital_CV_o1.txt*).

- Clean up the new file. Make sure that bullets convert properly. Add spaces between paragraphs to improve readability. Eliminate gaps within lines caused by tabs or indents.

- Save the changes in Notepad by clicking *File,* then *Save.*

Digital Design Rules

If you are preparing a new CV and want to make the fewest changes in formatting for digital, follow the suggestions below:

- Do not use shading and underlining.

- Do not use bold type. Try all caps for emphasis.

- Do not use italics.

- Do not use tables.

- Use only sans serif fonts – stick to plain-looking fonts without decorative squiggles, such as Arial and Helvetica.

- Do not use bullets. Asterisks or dashes will work fine.

- Do consider using a series of dashes (— — —) to separate sections.

Not every digital CV ends up being unseen by human eyes in the screening process. Many firms make it a practice to pass each CV to the computer screen of a recruiter on its way to the storage chambers. Unfortunately, that practice gets costly when companies are bombarded with thousands of superficial, misleading, or spammed CVs. The volume of irrelevant data skyrockets in tight employment markets, and the ability to provide a human review shrinks. This calls for aggressive action on your part to get directly to the right people with your information.

3. Paste your CV into an online format, such as a CV databank or a corporate hiring application.

- Launch Notepad (PC) and open your file (*my_digital_C_o1.txt*).

- For each field in the profile, select the appropriate text from your CV.

- Right-click the mouse and select *Copy*.

- Go to the web page. With the cursor blinking in the proper field on the web form, right-click and select *Paste*.

- Repeat the previous three steps for each of the profile fields you have to fill in. If you are pasting multiple keywords or terms on one line, place a comma after each term.

Harnessing the Power of E-mail

E-mail is the most powerful tool of the Internet. Here is a simple way to put it to use in your digital job search:

Use search engines to track down forums, professors, company managers, editors, and so on, until you get the names and e-mail addresses of several people in your field who will recognize your abilities. Send each of them a simple introductory e-mail. Begin by referring to something you know about them, or an article or paper you have read, or similar relevant comment. Pose a question important to you, such as: *Is there a particular industry job-listing site you recommend? What is the most up-to-date and reputable publication in the field? Is there a particular recruiting agency you recommend?*

Then provide five or six lines that provide an accurate picture of your talent. Thank them in advance for responding – and thank them again when they do. After receiving their response, honour it, and get back to them about what you did and what happened. Stay upbeat and avoid conveying any complaints about your search. If you have another question, ask it. If you need to puzzle something out, ask if you can call them.

When you develop a good and honest rapport, ask the person by e-mail if they would look at your CV – attached – to offer any leads or advice. Do not ask them to consider you for a job: They will do that on their own if they want to. People will help you with pleasure if they can. Most get uncomfortable if you press for advantage in their organization. If you plan to send the CV to the person's company and are qualified, tell them you are putting it through channels and ask them if there is anyone in particular they recommend you forward it to. Do so. If nothing happens, send your contact a short e-mail saying that you haven't heard back and will therefore assume there was no interest. Push no further – and wait to see if any advice comes along. Renew the contact a few months later.

Have several of these conversations going with each of your Job Targets.

PART FOUR

Person-to-Person Delivery

*N*one of the material in this book will do you any good unless someone reads your CV, someone who can make a positive decision to send you further along the hiring chain – ultimately to the final decision maker, who will give you an interview and then an offer. We emphasize read, since a lot of CVs get moved along the employment conveyor belt without ever getting serious consideration: they are simply sorted out, glanced at, filed for a later look, put in a hold file, stacked in a pile for fast prioritization – or just left sitting somewhere.

Employment itself involves a person-to-person relationship, and your job search must get to a person-to-person relationship before it delivers anything for you. This goes without saying, doesn't it? So how is it that so few job seekers take even the most basics steps to establish this critical personal contact? Many were never taught that it is OK to be assertive in their job search; others don't know how to; and some are convinced it won't make a difference, so they don't invest the time.

There is another reason too. People fear rejection, and the lack of response feels like less of a rejection. However, if you don't invest time and energy in the effort, if you don't go through a number of apparent and real rejections, you will not get to the 'Yes's, or will have to compromise your standards to get there. Plough on: the faster you get the 'No's out of the way, the faster you will get to the 'Yes's!

In the most practical sense, the CV's purpose is to get you an interview with the right person. Without the interview, no hiring will happen. That is why Part Four focuses on the delivery of your CV: getting it to the right person and making sure it is read and understood in a way that stimulates *that person's interest. Some of this recaps and expands on what you read in Parts One and Three. Parts Five and Six provide practical examples.*

Contents of Part Four

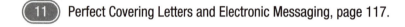

10

The Inside Track

Y ou have read about the complexities of Internet job searching in Chapter 3. Here is a detailed step-by-step method for using the Internet strategically to reach a particular person at a particular company to discuss the job you are after.

To make the most of the Internet, step away from the shortcuts and take an unconventional approach. Don't file your CV into a passive database or CV broadcasting service and sit around waiting for news. Reverse the logic and use the public and commercial job-search services, and good search-engine tactics, as a way of *identifying* the kind of job situations you are looking for – not applying for them. When you identify an opportunity that meets your criteria, rather than rush to fill out an electronic template or send a digital CV, instead, with that opening in mind, construct a strategy that will get you face to face with a real person who can make the hiring decision or influence it. Here is an expanded version of the five-step process referred to in Chapter 3.

Job Creation in Five Steps

1. **Start with specific Job Targets in mind.** It makes little sense to reach into the vast dimensions of the job market without a target of some specificity. You should probably have three or four specific

targets rather than lumping all of your options into one general objective. The more specific your Job Target, the more likely you are to locate corresponding opportunities and make a compelling case for yourself. A Job Target combines intersections of your skills and your interests, as you saw in Part Two. Once you have named your Job Targets, see how many different ways you can describe each job. Research the job descriptions and keywords you can use, and take time to look up variations on the jobs that interest you, then take those terms and put them into a search engine slot. The wealth of information available will amaze you.

2. **Identify specific locations where you desire to live and work.** To embark upon a national search when you really wouldn't consider moving out of London is a waste of time. Your most important search parameter is where you want to live. Choose a number of locations if you wish, as long as they are true possibilities for you even if a company wouldn't pay for relocation. (Some may, most won't, depending on the competition and the seniority of the job.) By researching each location separately, you capitalize on the benefits of proximity, local networking, and the ease of obtaining interviews with companies in the 'neighbourhood'.

3. **Get a list of *all* of the organizations in each location**, whether they have advertised jobs or not. It is easy. On your search engine, name the location with the words 'business directory', 'laboratory', 'small business directory', or a similar term. 'Manchester Business Directory' used as a search term will give you access to an amount of information no job-listing site will come close to, since job-listing sites carry only paid listings for open jobs. You, however, are looking way beyond that into the hidden job market. (In Chapter 3 you learned that a majority of companies with pending job openings do not advertise them until they have done their own internal networking.)

4. **Find out about organizations that appeal to you,** whether or not they have advertised open positions. Know their competitors, the industry, their products, and their financial condition as well as their mission and values and relationship to the community. Look

for people in the vicinity who might have contacts in the organization. Look for chamber of commerce affiliations, school boards, town hall, anywhere knowledgeable people might be who will talk to you.

5. **Get up close and personal.** Check the companies' websites to see what jobs are listed, if any. If you find a listing that matches your qualifications, don't respond immediately. Find a more personal means of access: with a few phone calls you can get the name of a person in the company (not necessarily in the recruitment role) who is connected to that position or knows someone whose job is related to it. Call the person directly, and send them an e-mail in advance of your CV. If there is no published job listing, assume there could be one in the future and do the same basic thing. Considering what you know about the firm and where you might fit in, call around and find someone who knows the area of your interest and ask for an opportunity to discuss future possibilities. Always stress the benefits you can bring to the enterprise – and organize your CV to reflect these benefits. Since you are doing several of these a week, in a short time you will have some productive conversations that will put you ahead of the curve.

What you did just above is called *job creation* – and it is one of the most powerful drivers of our economy. You can create your own job when you have a good understanding of what will help a company meet a challenge and communicate with the person looking for that solution. Where value is shown, opportunity opens. By using these assertive concepts, you step out of the realm of the obvious and competitive into the opportune.

Recap

Stop and think where you are going with this process:

1. You have assessed your skills, interests, and values and have a personal target worth the investment.

2. You have chosen one or more geographic locations that are right for you.

3. You have gone into the information infrastructure and learned what enterprises are located there.

4. You have extracted useful information for your career search.

5. You have made some good contacts for networking.

You are building a compelling case for how you will fit in and learning how to convince others of that. As you go through this research, you are always refining your ideas about your future career. Once this work is done, you will choose CV formats, keywords, and covering letter messages that communicate your case clearly.

In following this strategy you are not relying on a flawed system of overhyped job-finding services to manage your future. You are skillfully managing your career and your job search on your own terms.

More specifics on Internet CV research follow.

Digging Deeper Online

Good research allows you to go beyond the information on employment websites to the names of real people you can speak to one on one, by phone, in person, or via e-mail. These contacts will make a powerful supplement to your regular network of friends, colleagues, and co-workers.

Here are some good digging areas: search out whoever is writing and reporting in your target field. Use Internet search engines to find people, products, publications, associations, and company officers. Visit online forums to learn about new projects that trendsetters in the field are launching. If there is a company you are particularly interested in, look up them and their competitors in industry publications and online forums. These forums (text-based discussion groups) can be particularly valuable because past interactions are often archived. For example, Workforce.com has more than 30,000 subscribers who are practitioners in the HR field. Right there before your eyes are dozens of forums posing and answering questions about staffing, compensation, training, and other subjects of interest for people in that field.

By taking this non-conventional, research-oriented approach, you will get names, relevant employer concerns and issues, and e-mail addresses for professionals in the field. You will increase your interest and upgrade your knowledge of the subject before applying the information to your CV and covering letters. You are building the vocabulary of your future success. Just enter the name of your specialty and the word *forums* (as in 'geology forums') into a search engine, and you will find dozens of references to explore.

Going online, Cindi Moore located a child-care magazine she had not known about. She contacted the editor, who told her about several companies that provided training materials to the child-care field. She obtained appointments with three of these companies and is now working for one, a small company of fewer than twenty-five people. None of these firms had advertised or participated in online recruiting.

John North linked to some professional forums with wide participation from designers of health and beauty products. He read, thought, asked questions, got in contact with several participants, and found out what was going on in the field. He learned where the growth and demand were coming from and to whom his CV should go directly. He used this new material to customize his covering letters.

Don Sweet knew his field of hazardous waste removal well. He had been with one company for a dozen years and wanted to leave that firm and relocate. Before he put together his CV, he decided to assess himself against others in the industry. He subscribed to two of its many newsletters, found an editor who lived in the area, and arranged to meet her for lunch before starting his CV. She told him about the contracting problems some companies were facing and how they needed to build better relationships with the government agencies that were managing the programmes, or they might lose out. He had known about these problems, although not the companies that were involved. He saw where he could fit in and what he could do, and knew whom to contact to arrange a meeting. The letter and CV resulting from that meeting were focused on his contract-managing skills and experience.

He would have missed this opportunity had he not reached further than a simple job-search service.

Etiquette of Making Contacts: Do's and Don'ts

Do feel free to use e-mail when an address is public.

Do read the available materials first so you know in advance the questions you need to have answered.

Do use the contacts for getting leads and ideas, but **don't** put pressure on people to help you.

Do send thank-you e-mails to those whom you contact and let them know how you are doing. This is not only good manners, but also keeps the doors open for further communication.

Do be direct in asking the questions you want answers to. *Do you have the name of someone I could contact about that? Do you have her e-mail? May I use your name?*

Do use time well. Be brief and to the point.

Don't mislead or misrepresent.

Don't communicate your fears or plead for favours.

Don't let your nervousness get in the way. People tend to be far more receptive to requests for information than most of us realize.

11

Perfect Covering Letters and Electronic Messaging

As you write, edit, and format your CV, you may polish it to a high sheen, but it will still be a generalized, impersonal communication. This is especially true with the pigeonholing that comes with keywording, as you try to fit your marketable skills into search-engine vocabularies. Just as most company job descriptions tell you little about the culture, projects, and working style of an enterprise, most conventional CVs and covering letters, which are generalized to minimize preparation time or get the widest distribution, become like commodities.

There is no software on the horizon that can outdo one-on-one communication. And that is where a good letter comes in – the favourite and most powerful communication form in history. The best letters have something to say that hits the reader personally. Every marketing expert says emphatically that the closer you can get to your customer in style, voice, and content, the more business you will conduct. So why would you *not* want to send a personal communication to any firm you would consider working for?

Ever since mass-market digital job banks increased in importance with their templates and slots, there has been a declining use of customized covering letters – because they are too human to fit into the automated system. Ironically, this decline in use is one reason to use a distinctive covering letter: it is one of the few remaining ways to make your singular mark as a person and to shape the hiring process to your own needs and objectives. A customized covering letter is essential for the best jobs in your world.

What Is a Customized Covering Letter?

A customized covering letter is an individualized communication addressed to a specific person – by name, not title – that makes them want to find out more about you in filling announced and un-announced positions in the company. It is often sent by e-mail, preferably as an attachment, and sometimes by regular post or an expedited delivery service. It offers you these unique and important benefits:

Voice

Throughout history, letter writing has given people a way to be heard. By its tone, character, and vocabulary, a letter conveys the feeling of a personal conversation with the sender. On a digitalized, scanned, keyworded CV, you have no voice. You are printed out as a set of specs like an invoice or purchase order. But with a letter that you have authored, your identity finds its way into the reader's mind like a character rising from the pages of a novel. Write with personal style.

EXAMPLES:

CONFIDENT, UPBEAT
I saw the good news about your award. Congratulations! It should also be helpful to your Boeing project – *Aviation Week* certainly wrote glowingly about that!

TECHNICAL
My skills in non-linear programming and mathematical distortion should prove valuable to your new work. Probability modelling in particular will introduce many advantages in structuring your tests. My paper on the subject might be of interest to you. A link is attached for your convenience. If you

would like to view my full technical portfolio/CV, please let me know.

STRATEGIC

This is an enquiry sent before a possible application with Raytheon Systems. I've watched with interest the research and development leadership your company has assumed, as simple GPS has evolved to onboard multi-variable precision navigation. I would like to consider opportunities at your company, should I qualify.

However, before I send out a CV and perhaps waste your time, there are two concerns I need to address. Are people working on a PhD (as I am) allowed to take certain amounts of time off for thesis work? Do you encourage participation in scientific conferences on related subjects? These are important considerations in my future planning, so I hope you do not mind my bringing them up in advance.

I look forward to receiving your answers. I've attached a list of preliminary qualifications and will be happy to send a full CV when appropriate.

Relationship

In any good letter, you are speaking person to person, one to one. In the language of the letter, you are setting up your relationship with the reader. Are you a supplicant, colleague, potential partner, or peer? Are you making an offer or asking for a favour? The way you write the letter will establish this initial relationship.

EXAMPLES:

I would very much appreciate the opportunity to discuss some of these matters with you and your colleagues personally. Can we schedule a phone call?

It would be professionally exciting to work with your team on this project. I know that Ford is noted for its teamwork models around Six Sigma.

We have something in common: the belief that the customer comes first. I read your article in last June's *Wharton School Quarterly* and found it to be very powerful, especially when compared with similar work from others.

Scope

Even with the best natural-language programming or semantic interpreters, there is no scanning software available that can understand the scope of capability you offer to a work situation. Most search engines can only slice, define, count, add, subtract, and score. Screened out are precisely those terms you might need to define the scope of your capability. Words such as *breakthrough, quantum leap, invention, creative, expressive, major,* and *minor* don't even show up.

How, for example, can you define in a CV the size and complexity of problems you took on when you transformed losses to gains in customer satisfaction indexes across a dealer network? Instead, we are back to 'years of experience' as the measure of a person's scope. Back to haunt us is that old adage that a person who has one year of experience sixteen years over has sixteen years' experience. With your letter, you can show that your experience actually exceeds your years.

EXAMPLES:

Although the exact numbers are proprietary, this was a very big win for the company and was widely credited with bringing that division well into the black for the first time in three years.

Through my staff, I interacted with over two dozen field reps in this launch, and the breakthrough earnings caused the company to use the launch as a model for future promotions.

Each of my three main clients retained my services for more than five years, a major feat considering the volatility of that market segment.

Individuality

Most company job-listing sites ask you to be sure to include the file number of the job you are applying for – otherwise they won't process you. You go from being an individual to a CV to server mincemeat, and then you're screened through lots of filters by clerks and given the verdict: accept for investigation, consider later, hold, invite, delete. Who are you, really? That's hard to say. The customized covering letter, if well done, will reconstitute you as a unique individual.

EXAMPLES:
Few industrial lighting-fixture sales reps have a fine arts degree, but it has given me a special rapport with the top-tier clients.

It was valuable and motivating to bring together my skills as a public opinion researcher at Marist and my longtime interests in community planning in such a high-profile way (article attached). I am looking for the opportunity to do something even larger next time.

After one or two attempts there was heavy pressure to pull back, but the risks we took soon produced major pay-offs – and now those methods are becoming commonplace in the industry. I am not risk averse, nor am I foolhardy.

Legitimacy

With agencies bundling thousands of CVs together each day and sending them out to thousands of commercial placement agencies and spam CV generators, companies are increasingly suspicious of what they get. Is this a person looking for a free interview trip to a holiday location? Are his credentials fictitious? Does she have pseudo-job searches going at dozens of other firms, including competitors? Or is she really as good as she appears? A customized covering letter makes you real and tangible. The better the letter, the more memorable your CV is and the more legitimate you are.

I am well aware of the huge numbers of people hitting your company with CVs as you grow. I'm sending this to you personally to assure you my credentials are authentic. For further verification, feel free to contact my colleague John Simmons, who I understand is known to you from your time as a student at Wye College.

In sending you this CV, I am assuring you that you are the only company I have enquired about so far, as you are my first choice. I will widen my search if I don't hear from you within a week.

Enquiry

The most respected job seekers are often those who have the best questions to ask. To answer a question, the reader has to engage their mind, which puts you squarely into their field of attention. And their response will let you know if this is the kind of place you want to work. It may also result in their reshaping their idea of what the job entails. This is not difficult to accomplish if you can generate the right combination of questions and responses – in other words, kick off a dialogue. It can start with your letter.

EXAMPLES:

I found the digital job descriptions on your site to be generalized, which I'm sure was intentional. My area of marketing is not as well known as many, and I would like to know more about what you are looking for before I send my CV. Could you tell me a bit more about the results you are looking for, and how you plan to measure them? This will give me the opportunity to be more focused in my response to you. Thank you.

I have been a heavy producer in this field for five years. Would it be possible for me to discuss the key factors of this job opening before applying for it with my rather general CV? This will give you a better picture of my potential value.

Action

In a CV, there is no room to request a specific action. A call for action is a legitimate part of a customized covering letter, and it calls for an answer. Most CVs submitted today are not responded to. Customized covering letters greatly increase your chances of getting a response.

EXAMPLES:

If a personal conversation is possible, please let me know what time is convenient for you. Thank you.

One of my rare trips to Edinburgh is coming up in two weeks, and this would be an excellent time for us to meet or for me to talk to one of your staff. I will be there for business on 17 March. I can keep the next day free if you wish.

Although it may be presumptuous of me to do so, I will phone your office next week to see if what I suggest is possible. Thank you for your time and attention.

CV Spotlight

One common function the covering letter serves is to point the reader's attention to specific parts of the CV that apply to a particular opportunity, and to add clarification to items in your CV if necessary. This allows one basic CV to be used multiple times.

EXAMPLES:

As you will see from my CV, much of my recent work has been with non-profit groups. I'd like to emphasize that my work in these organizations was driven towards budget and return on funding. I am no stranger to making sure that every initiative has a strong financial return.

Thank you for taking the time to read my CV. You will see my general reference to digital graphics in the section about my skills. To expand on this, I'd like you to know that I am highly capable with Illustrator, Photoshop, In Design, and

PageMaker. Since these are tools that are used in your design shop, my skills should be valuable in your office. I have an online portfolio of my work. If you would like to review it, link to www.dsp.com/port.

Putting Your Letter Together

First of all, know by name the person to whom you want to send the letter, along with their e-mail or postal address. A letter to just a title, or an e-mail without a name, loses impact. The person you want to send the letter to is the person who would normally make or influence the hiring decision – not a personnel officer, but a manager or division head. There are several ways to get this valuable information.

- If you know the division or department you are interested in, phone the company and ask for the manager of that department and speak to their secretary. Or phone a company office described in an annual report or other public document and ask a secretary in that office for the name of the person holding the position you want to reach. Note the spelling carefully, then ask for the e-mail address and the phone extension for future direct contact.

- Make certain you are accurately spelling the person's name, their position, and the company. You will get off on the wrong foot fast if you get those wrong, especially if the job is detail oriented.

- Be prepared. If you are connected directly to the person you had wanted to e-mail, just say that you are planning to send them an e-mail and are calling now to verify their name and address. It is better at this stage to get your ideas together by e-mail than leap right into a conversation. However, if there is a conversation, say something like, 'I am considering opportunities at your company, but before I apply, there are a few questions I would like to ask, and I'd like to e-mail them to you.' If *they* want to hear the questions right away, you can ask such things as, '*Is this a growing area at the company?*' '*Are there any good trade journal articles I can read about the company?' 'Does the company do the work itself or is it outsourced?'* As you speak, use the person's name. Don't panic and ask for a job. Strategically build the relationship first. Don't forget to mention this conversation when you send your e-mail. Send it the next day if possible.

Once again, another good source of names to contact at a particular division of a company is search engines. For example, say you have an MBA and want to get into GE Capital because they are located where you want to live and are a big player in the field. Get on Google or your favourite search engine and type in 'GE Capital products'. This will take you to a financial products page showing the different services they provide. Choose one or two to review. (Remember, you are not searching anywhere near the careers page – you're where their customers go.) You will find press releases and lots of detail, including recent deals, quotes from real people by name, e-mail addresses, and, by implication, the kinds of skills they are looking for and where their business is headed. You can spend an hour and come up with a dozen real live contacts.

It's even simpler than that at times. Say you want to work in a small web-design firm in Croydon, Surrey. On Google, type in the terms 'Web design Croydon Surrey', hit 'enter', and you'll retrieve around 82,000 sites. Try it and see! Choose one, and on the web page you should find information and contacts. It has never been easier than this.

If you are e-mailing both a covering letter and a CV at the same time, it is important to make sure that they don't get separated, as will often happen if your covering letter is in the e-mail message and your CV is an attachment. This calls for a referral message in the body of the e-mail: *Given your interest in structured finance, I invite you to see the attached covering letter and CV.* Then have the covering letter and CV as part of the same attached document with a page or section break to separate them. If you want to put your covering letter in the e-mail, that's OK, but repeat it in the attachment.

If you have done the preliminary work, there are many ways to personalize your approach to the job you want and increase your odds of getting it. If you have not taken the time for research, you lose these advantages.

No matter how you prepare and deliver your covering letter, edit it carefully and use a formal letterhead layout – with name, address, phone number, and e-mail. If you are sending it by post, use good paper, such as a quality cotton-fibre type (quality papers specially intended for this purpose are available from stationers). As in the case of dressing for the interview, appearance counts. Also don't forget to get each letter edited.

Sample Covering Letter

CARL GOODRICH
387 SOUTH PARK DRIVE
CROYDON, CR9 3JT
(020) 8686 3322
carlgood@internetprovider.co.uk

23 May, 2004

Mr. Donald M. Wasserman
Wasserman, Hinkle and Associates
50 Hyde Park Boulevard

Dear Mr. Wasserman,

Makes connection

It was a pleasure meeting you last weekend at the Charles Schwab presentation. Your client list seems outstanding and I believe my current clients could fit into your portfolio management style well.

Communicates strengths and benefit

I have had an impeccable career with Croydon Council. However, my best accomplishments in the past several years were in earning an MA in Finance and building successful client relationships as a licensed investment adviser. This would be an exciting career transition for me as I already have a good track record in my freelance work. The first page of my CV highlights my specific accomplishments freelancing as well as my work with the state agency.

Requests action

I'm still employed by the council and can't be reached at work from Monday afternoon through Thursday. However I'm available after work by phone and e-mail and can meet you on Friday afternoons or Monday mornings. I'll phone you next Monday to see when we can meet.

Thank you,

Carl Goodrich
Carl Goodrich

RECAP:

- Decide on the purpose of your covering letter.

- Decide whom you are going to send it to by name and how you are going to get it to them.

- Introduce yourself.

- Make your point – your Selling Case.

- Ask for a response.

- Thank the reader for their time.

- Follow up with a phone call two or three days from receipt.

Covering Letter Organizer

Answer the following questions to organize the content of your letter. Then use your answers to compose the letter. Regarding a specific company, department, or need:

- Who is the right person to reach?

- What is the problem or concern you might help solve?

- How can you assist the employer right away?

- What have you accomplished that demonstrates your added value to this employer?

- How will the employer specifically benefit from hiring you?

- What is the 'call to action' you are asking for?

Paragraph Suggestions

Read these over and select any that are useful to you as a guide to help you write your covering letter. Refer back to your Selling Case on page 43 and other material in Part Two.

OPENING PARAGRAPHS

I saw the _____ position your company listed on [website's] job board and am submitting my CV directly to you so I can highlight my particular competencies in this work. In my _____ years with _____ in the [department] as a _____, I've developed particular (qualities/skills/needs) I believe will significantly help you meet your goal of _____.

According to [internal contact/company newsletter, external contact], I understand you are considering [goals, projects, direction] and could be in the market for someone who can provide strong leadership in pursuit of this goal.

The article in [company newsletter/external publication/business press] about your [department/firm] was impressive. Congratulations. I'm pleased to see you get recognition for your commitment to _____.

[Internal contact/external contact] suggested that since my background is in _____, I get in touch with you to discuss how I can best contribute to your [department's/company's] work in _____.

As an employee of _____ in the [department], I'm well aware of your [department's/company's] strong reputation in _____ and _____.

I have been following your [department's/company's] progress in _____ for _____ years and believe the skills I've developed while working at _____ in the [department] will make a significant contribution towards meeting your goals.

I saw the [notice/job posting/advertisement] for a part-time position as a _____ and wish to express my interest and enthusiasm in transferring the _____ skills I developed in my current position as a _____ at _____.

I admire your work as a leader in the field of _____. I have been following your progress in _____ for _____ years.

MAIN BODY PARAGRAPH
(Also review the examples earlier in this chapter.)

I believe that with your [department's/company's] reputation as a
_____, and my fresh insight into _____, I could make a
significant contribution right away by _____.

With my background in _____ and _____ I believe my
unique skills would promote [the company's] continued growth and
success by _____.

I am someone who can _____ with customers who _____.
I believe I would make a noticeable difference [in your department/at
your company] by _____.

Because I have _____ years of experience in _____, I
think my _____ skills will help meet your [department's/
company's] need to _____.

Since my background is in _____, [internal contact/external
contact] believes I could be a valuable contributor to your [depart-
ment's/company's] objectives of _____.

I share your interest in _____ and offer my _____ skills to
match your need for a _____. What would make this unique for
both of us is _____, as you will see in my CV, where I
summarize _____.

Now that I have completed advanced [training/education] and
received my _____, I believe that in combination with my
_____ years as a _____ at _____, I can offer a more
up-to-the-minute capability than ever to your [department/company].

While my hourly commitment would not be full time, the experience
and skills in _____ and _____ I can bring to the position
will reflect my successes in the field of _____.

For the past _____ years, I have worked as a _____ with
[department/company]. During this time, I have acquired experience
in _____ and earned recognition for _____.

I am especially proud of _____, which will be reflected in the results I can bring to your company.

My involvement in _____ has provided opportunities to practise the skills of _____ and _____. I realize these capabilities are important to a [department/company] like yours that excels in _____.

In my career as a _____, I have had the opportunity to hone my problem-solving skills. In particular, I've learned how to facilitate _____ and _____. These abilities prove essential when faced with _____.

As a _____, I feel I have two unique benefits to offer to you: _____ and _____. Throughout my career, these qualities have produced an increase in _____. They have also encouraged others to _____.

I know that a _____ has to have the quality of _____, and I know that quality is important to your [department/company]. It's a characteristic I've worked on throughout my career.

Throughout my career, I have continuously improved my ability to _____. The results in _____ have won acclaim from _____.

In my experience with _____, I've had to learn new _____ and _____ thoroughly. If training in _____ and _____ are necessary for success with your [department/company], then I'm ready.

When I was _____, I developed a successful _____. This important project brought my [department/company] a _____ per cent increase in sales. After studying your [department/company], I feel that I could achieve similar results after a period of _____.

Although it has been several years since I worked directly with _____, I believe my ability to _____ and _____ added to other skills will prove extremely valuable. The new opening sounds like a perfect opportunity to combine these skills as a _____ in your [department/company].

CLOSING PARAGRAPH

I am confident my knowledge and abilities would be of value to your [department/company]. I request a few minutes of your time to discuss my qualifications and ask a few questions. I will contact your office on _____ to possibly arrange a phone meeting. If you have any questions in the meantime, please phone or e-mail me.

I know your time is valuable; however, I would like a few minutes to discuss the above qualifications and how they might directly benefit your [department/organization]. I will contact you on _____ to set up a meeting. Please call me if you have any questions.

Your commitment to _____ and my experience in _____ look like a strong match. I'm sure this relationship could be good for the growth of [department/company]. After you have had time to review my CV, I will contact you about meeting to discuss future possibilities.

I would appreciate a chance to meet you and discuss how my skills could assist your [department/company] in its goal to _____. I will be in the area on _____ and will phone you on _____ to see if there is a convenient time we can meet during my stay. If this time won't work for you, please e-mail me at _____.

Note: In these closing paragraph suggestions you are encouraged to keep the initiative in your court. Although this might seem like an imposition, it is usually the best way to ensure that the contact happens. Far too many applicants leave the ending open and then wait and wait – never knowing if they will be hearing from the recipient. When you assert that you are going to call, this keeps you on your toes (note your diary and call when you say you will), and the employer generally moves more quickly to consider your message.

PART FIVE

Success Stories

*T*he following pages feature five different people, each with a story of how they made career choices and changes. Their stories have been chosen to enable you to understand the thoughts and strategies behind what they did and see the materials they wrote to support their career moves. There are CVs, covering letters, internal proposals, and other documents.

A short synopsis:

Success Story 1 Cynthia Spencer has a twenty-five-year work history that includes a business career, a career in education, and freelance work. We follow her as she pursues three different Job Targets at the same time. Included: three CVs, three covering letters, and a philosophy 'white paper' she sent with one CV. (Page 137)

Success Story 2 Arianna Corbuski had to relocate when her husband was promoted to a job in another city. She had to change industries, but kept the same function. Included: two CVs, one for her current industry and one translated to fit the new industry. (Page 154)

Success Story 3 Cornell French suffered from a mental disability that – with accommodations – would not disturb the quality of his work. His story shows how he negotiated these accommodations in his job campaign. Included: commendation letter (reference) and his CV. (Page 160)

Success Story 4 Marilyn and Donna combined their talents in a successful job share, each working half time. Included: 'CV for two' and a covering letter. (Page 167)

CYNTHIA SPENCER'S STORY

TWENTY-FIVE YEARS IN THE WORKFORCE AND STILL MAKING CHANGES

Cynthia is a divorced woman in her late forties. She graduated from Columbia University in 1978 with a Master of Fine Arts (MFA) degree in theatre education, and had a BA in English from the University of Texas at Austin.

After earning her master's degree, Cynthia spent three years writing advertising copy for a New York City agency. She spent the next three years working for the Department of Social Services in Dallas.

In the mid-eighties, Cynthia joined her husband's business performance consulting company, Hanover Associates. Her husband introduced her to performance coaching, and together they built a successful business. When they divorced in 1996, Cynthia created the High Performers Corporation with a business partner. This business was similar to Hanover, but focused on selling software manuals and other materials rather than on in-person performance coaching. The flexibility of her new business gave Cynthia the time to develop a part-time teaching career. She spent three years as an adjunct professor of English.

Following a downturn in the economy there was a glut of consultants desperate for work. Cynthia's business began to flag and she lost interest in trying to keep it going. She asked a career counsellor to review her skills and past experience. Together, they came up with three Job Targets:

1. A full-time job, working with a corporate consulting firm

2. Two part-time jobs: teaching online plus regular classroom teaching of the same subject (for the same private college)

3. Full-time lecturer (community college)

Each of these three job targets drew on a different but equally valuable aspect of her skills and experience. Each required its own CV and covering letter strategy.

For Job Target 1, you'll see a covering letter and then a two-page chronological CV. After you read through those three pages, look to the next page for an explanation for her choices.

For Job Target 2, you'll see a covering letter accompanying a two-page targeted CV. Again, the final page explains the thinking behind how she put her information together.

For Job Target 3, there's a covering letter responding to an ad, a copy of the ad, an excerpt of the CV, a partial document of a white paper asked for in the ad, all followed by the rationale.

CYNTHIA SPENCER
5362 Holliston Road
Fredericksburg, TX 12345
555-123-4567
CS@internetprovider.com

24 April, 2004
Ms. Tyler Courveaux
President, North America
BBK World Headquarters
1500 Susquehanna Lake Road
Dallas, TX 12345

Dear Ms. Courveaux,

I was delighted to read of BBK's history of success. A few years ago, your company and ours were partnered in a performance coaching assignment for Marshall Fields' buying offices in Houston. BBK handled the executives, and we worked with the middle managers. Our company was Hanover Corp.

As you will see from my CV, I was quite active in performance coaching in the early nineties. By 2000, my business partner and I moved into marketing software and other web-based performance materials.

In this latest business I also had time to use other talents: teaching college English and heading the board of directors for two community service organizations. My best skills are: group facilitation, including teaching; coaching in communications skills; and writing and editing. I have recently dissolved High Performers Corp and wish to return to performance counselling and/or group facilitation as a full-time consultant.

I would love to come to Dallas and meet you briefly. I'll phone to check your availability for a meeting. I hope your business continues to go well. Performance coaching has become much more competitive in the past decade. BBK's success story is an inspiration.

Respectfully,

Cynthia Spencer

CYNTHIA SPENCER
5362 Holliston Road
Fredericksburg, TX 12345
555-123-4567
CS@internetprovider.com

OBJECTIVE: Performance Coaching for Managers and Executives

SUMMARY: Fifteen years of delivery and development experience in the areas of performance coaching and career development for managers and executives.

Co-authored two books, published by AMA, *Performance Plus* (2000); *Performance First* (1999).

WORK HISTORY:

2000–present   HIGH PERFORMERS CORP. Fredericksburg, TX
                         Vice-president, Programme Development and Delivery

- Wrote and edited content for interactive software, training manuals, and workbooks for performance development.
- Developed work performance website called performanceplus.com, including writing and editing performance counsellor case history material and a downloadable 104-page book on coaching for high performance for managers and supervisors.

1990–2000   HANOVER CORPORATION, San Antonio, TX
                         Executive Vice-president, Co-Owner

- Programme Developer, Workshop Leader for both national and international corporate clients, including IBM, General Motors Corp, Citibank, Tyson Foods, Marshall Fields' Buying Offices, the Rand Corporation.
- Trained a dozen workshop leaders who delivered training material to thousands of managers worldwide.
- Counselled over one hundred executives to enhance personal performance; overall success rate was 30–45 per cent employee performance improvement.
- Led numerous group workshops as large as 100 and as small as 10: executives, middle managers, and union leaders.

Cynthia Spencer   555-123-4567   CS@internetprovider.com

OTHER AREAS OF WORK AND INTEREST

1999–2002   MONROE COLLEGE, San Antonio, TX

Taught College Writing 1 & 2, and devoted hundreds of hours to tutoring students in writing and communication.
Adjunct Professor of English

1997–present SHARE THE WEALTH, Fredericksburg, TX

Helped direct Not-for-Profit social service agency delivering 17 human services programmes, serving Waco and San Antonio Counties
President, Board of Directors

2002–2004   ACTOR'S PLAY GROUP, Fredericksburg, TX

Helped launch improvisational theatre company affiliated with the International Theater Games Company
President, Board of Directors

PUBLISHED WORK

Co-authored with Dr. Terence Balfour:
Performance Plus (American Management Association, 2000)
Performance First (American Management Association, 1999)

EDUCATION

Current   Online coursework in fiction writing
MFA   Columbia University, New York, NY
BA   University of Texas at Austin

Commentary on Cynthia's Choices
JOB TARGET 1

Covering Letter

This is a networking, informal letter, with no advertised job.

1. **Opening paragraph** Cynthia's compliment is genuine: BBK's success is obvious from their website. Cynthia reminds her reader that she already has a connection with the company. They had both worked for the same client over ten years ago (she says a few years ago).

2. **Second paragraph** Cynthia acknowledges an outstanding career in performance coaching with no apology for the fact that she's been away from it for the past five years.

3. **Third paragraph** She delineates her strongest marketable skills that fit the reader's potential needs. She says she dissolved her company without going into the reasons why.

4. **Closing paragraph** She asks for a meeting and promises to call. And she acknowledges the company's success a second time.

Chronological CV

1. **Objective and Summary** Cynthia accounts for no more than fifteen years, although her work history goes back over twenty and includes start-up jobs unrelated to her overall career and her current objectives. She flags her most relevant accomplishments here and repeats them again later.

2. **Chronological History** She goes back only fifteen years, selecting only the most salient outcomes and responsibilities. Her High Performers history indicates it's still present day, even though she's dissolving the business.

3. **Other Areas of Work and Interest** Here she includes part-time work and voluntary activity that demonstrates her professional community standing and broad range of skills, all potentially appealing and relevant to this employer contact.

4. **Published Work** She repeats this highly relevant accomplishment in its own category.

5. **Education** She gives no dates and does not say what her degree was in either university. Her universities are noteworthy, but her degree specialty is no longer relevant to her career as it evolved over the years.

Cynthia Spencer
5362 Holliston Road
Fredericksburg, TX 12345
111-234-5678
CS@internetprovider.com

12 August, 2004

Dr. Howard LeRoy
Dean, School of Graduate and Continuing Education
Monroe College
9876 South Road
San Antonio, TX 12345

Dear Dr. LeRoy,

My friend Dr. Joe Salzerullo suggested I contact you regarding possible openings on your online learning courses. I taught three years part time at Monroe from 1999 to 2002 as an Adjunct Professor of English, teaching College Writing 1 and 2. By early 2002 I had my own consulting partnership designing materials and leading workshops on performance coaching for organizations. The travel schedule subsumed the teaching schedule, so I reluctantly left teaching in May 2002.

For the last year our focus has moved strongly to the Internet. We created a website that sells performance manuals and other interactive products. Now we work online with customers and I can tune in at my own pace. Since I'm no longer travelling, I'm free to return to my first love – teaching.

I enclose my CV, which briefly highlights my work history and skills. I have a good reputation as a teacher from my work at Monroe, and my current online experience is a plus for your web-based programme.

I am available for the Spring 2005 term and would like to explore online teaching opportunities with you. It's likely that I will pick up a class or two from Dr. Salzerullo on campus in January, teaching College Writing.

If you have a free moment in the next couple of weeks, I'd like to meet you to discuss my becoming a member of your Adult Ed Team. I'll phone soon. Dr. Salzerullo can give you a first reference.

Many thanks,

Cynthia Spencer

CYNTHIA SPENCER
5362 Holliston Road
Fredericksburg, TX 12345
111-234-5678
CS@internetprovider.com

JOB TARGET: Online Instructor, College Writing 1 & 2
School of Graduate and Continuing Education

CAPABILITIES:

- Develop curriculum to fit a wide range of reading interests and writing skills.
- Create rapport with every student in every class by establishing levels of their success through their willingness to participate with professor and each other.
- Establish a love of reading and writing through frequent small assignments and in-depth discussion. Examples: short fiction, literary essays.
- Available 24/7 (by e-mail) for questions and upgrades to assigned work.
- Tutor students for any and all assignments, including term papers, CVs and covering letters, theses, and critical analysis assignments.

ACHIEVEMENTS:

- Developed progressive innovative curriculum over three years teaching college writing students at Monroe College.
- Tutored over 100 students in the Monroe Writing Center over three years. This included film analysis papers, critical analysis of literature and non-fiction, graduating senior theses.
- Established excellent rapport with ESL students. Became their tutor of choice.
- Co-authored two books published by the AMA: *Performance Plus* (2000) and *Performance First* (1999).
- Edited four published books in the business management field.
- Wrote and edited 100 pages of performance enhancement advice for commercial website (2004).
- Conducted a successful fiction writing group for five years (1996–2001).

WORK EXPERIENCE:

2000–present   HIGH PERFORMERS CORP. Fredericksburg, TX
Writer, Editor, Administrator

Wrote and edited content for interactive software, and content for training manuals and workbooks for performance workshops. Served as Management Adviser for seven years. Currently writing web content.

1999–2002 MONROE COLLEGE, San Antonio, TX
Adjunct Professor of English – College Writing 1 and 2
Tutor in the Writing Center
Supervisor: Dr. Joseph Salzerullo

1990–2000 HANOVER CORPORATION, San Antonio, TX
Programme Developer, Workshop Leader for both national and international corporate clients, including IBM, General Motors Corp., Citibank: trained a dozen workshop leaders who delivered training material to thousands of managers worldwide.

PUBLISHED WORK:

Co-authored with Dr. Terence Balfour:
Performance Plus (American Management Association, 2000)
Performance First (American Management Association, 1999)

EDUCATION   MFA Columbia University, New York, NY
BA University of Texas at Austin

ONGOING DEVELOPMENT

- Online courses in writing non-fiction from:
  University of Missouri at Columbia, School of Journalism
- Continuous workshops and memberships with AMA

Commentary on Cynthia's Choices

JOB TARGET 2

Covering Letter

1. **Opening paragraph** This is a direct referral from someone who knows both Cynthia and her employer contact. Her referral strongly believes there is an opening for a job (part-time) and has already used her services at the same institution. Cynthia establishes her successful connection to the college and a good reason for being absent from teaching the past three years.

2. **Second paragraph** Cynthia explains in simple terms her transition away from corporate work, her establishment of a business, and how it has added to her Internet capability.

3. **Third paragraph** Here Cynthia states what a CV can't (it also happens to be true and can easily be checked out with her reference): she left a good track record at the school, and her latest business skills add to what she can now offer to teaching. She asks for the job, and discloses she'll already be working part time on campus. She asks for a meeting and flags her reference beforehand, since he knows both of them.

The Targeted CV

1. **Job Target** This is very precise. She knows beforehand there is a possible opening and this title is the job's own.

2. **Capabilities** Every single statement is fully focused on this particular job. She has researched and understood the specific outcomes the job requires. Her most important sales pitch is the first line under capabilities. Developing curriculum is the first skill she must have to teach distance learning to a mostly adult group.

3. **Achievements** Previous success at Monroe comes first. Other writing achievements follow. Note there is nothing from her corporate work listed, which in itself is credible and admirable, but *not for this employer target*.

4. **Work Experience** Again, she goes back only fifteen years. She still accounts for her corporate work, but gives equal weight to teaching, even though it was part time.

5. **Published Work** This is given equal importance with teaching (skills) and corporate training (content).

6. **Education and Ongoing Development** Again, no dates, no degrees. Her history and credentials are enough.

CYNTHIA SPENCER
5362 Holliston Road
Fredericksburg, TX 12345
555-123-4567
CS@internetprovider.com

11 February, 2004

Human Resources Management
Southwest Community College
35 Howell Road
San Antonio, TX 12345

Re: the full-time temporary position teaching Developmental Composition, Autumn 2004. San Antonio News, 10 February, 2004

Greetings!

As you will see from my CV I have had a full career in leading groups, part-time college teaching, and writing and editing business-related material as well as co-authoring two published books.

Of all my work, however, teaching composition at Monroe College was the most fulfilling. I am drawn to the various cultures in your student body. Although Monroe included many privileged students, there were plenty who struggled with learning disabilities and other debilitating handicaps, as well as foreign students who only wanted someone to listen to them carefully enough to 'get' what they were attempting to say (or write). These were my greatest successes, producing the deepest form of personal fulfillment.

My assignments with High Performers Corp. are freelance, and I will be available for full-time work by June 2004. I hope we can meet and talk.

Sincerely,

Cynthia Spencer

CYNTHIA SPENCER
5362 Holliston Road
Fredericksburg, TX 12345
555-123-4567
CS@internetprovider.com

JOB TARGET: Lecturer/ Developmental Composition, Professor of English, Writing

CAPABILITIES:

- Develop creative curriculum to fit a wide range of writing styles
- Create rapport with every student in every class by establishing individual levels of success and encouraging them to interact verbally
- Establish a love of reading and writing through frequent small assignments and in-depth discussion. Examples: advertising
- Available 24/7 (by e-mail) for questions and upgrades to assigned work
- Tutor students for any and all assignments, including term papers, CVs and covering letters, theses, and critical analysis assignments

ACHIEVEMENTS:

- Developed progressive innovative curriculum over three years teaching college writing students at Monroe College

Cynthia Spencer

5362 Holliston Road
Fredericksburg, TX 12345
555-123-4567
CS@internetprovider.com

MY TEACHING PHILOSOPHY

There are three essential aspects to good teaching: passionate love of the subject matter, an uncompromising commitment to those I teach, and the skill and flexibility to go to any length within reason to make the subject matter come alive.

This is, of course, in addition to a strong and continuously growing knowledge of English grammar, spelling, and punctuation; and of writing styles, learning styles, reading methods, and analytical approaches, as well as an appreciation for language development, including word origins.

My approach to teaching writing is first to debunk the assumption that anyone knows how to write reasonably well upon leaving high school. Most high school writing, even among the best students, is pedantic at best, clumsy and confusing at worst. When I first meet my classes at the beginning of a term, I establish that the classes will be interactive, so that we both know we're 'here'. Students get credit for speaking up, whether they're right or wrong. No one is ever embarrassed or humiliated for making a bad guess.

We spend the first two classes on observation. Without observation, college writers go too directly into technique, of which they know very little at first. This is learning to walk before you can run.

To learn observation we take field trips to unusual places, usually right on campus, like visiting a construction area, touching and examining unknown objects, taking notes on all the senses operating during the field trip. No one is allowed to talk. When we return we have an oral report from notes. The first assignment is to write a short essay (expository) on any aspect of the field trip experience.

Another typical class is to pair up every student and assign each team to prepare a stand-up 'inspiring' presentation on some of the dullest and most difficult chapters from a collection of handbooks used in college writing classes. Of course, the students are not left on their own. I challenge them during their presentation to defend their lesson, which is usually quite a bit of fun, as they are forced to make sense of what they're saying and try to learn at the same time. Students like to listen to each other more than to the teacher, but, of course, my guiding hand and knowledge are ever present.

The bottom line in my philosophy is to instill within the minds and hearts of those I teach that they must respect their own experience and their ability to think and discern truth from lies. I've often set up debates when we touch on a controversial subject. [Continues onto a second page, not presented here.]

Commentary on Cynthia's Choices

JOB TARGET 3

Covering Letter

1. **Opening paragraph** Before the heading she notes the purpose of the letter, referring to the ad in the *San Antonio News*. This is a must when answering an ad. She says 'Greetings', rather than 'Dear sir or madam'. She summarizes her writing and teaching skills and directs the reader to examine them further in her CV.

2. **Second paragraph** Here she answers to the criteria required in the ad by explaining how she did teach a diverse student body, even though her experience was in a private college with students from more privileged backgrounds than those at the school to which she was applying. In fact, she admits that her proudest accomplishments were with those students who had the biggest struggles. High capability with students struggling to learn was her unique selling proposition.

3. **Third paragraph and closing** She flags the fact that her current work will be complete in time to take on a full-time lecturer's position. She makes no promise to call, but in fact she did anyway.

Targeted CV

1. **Job Target** This is exactly what the ad in the paper stated.

2. **Capabilities** Cynthia used the exact same CV as she did for the online part-time teaching job. They called for the same skills.

3. **Achievements** Again she used all the same information from the other targeted CV.

Essay on Teaching Philosophy

This is sometimes called a 'white paper' and is especially suggested for people entering a field of which they have a thorough understanding, but usually little or no direct experience. In this case, Cynthia wrote about real direct experience and details of how she most successfully taught during her three years of part-time college teaching. She gave the kind of detail one just wouldn't make up, and also demonstrates an unconventional approach to teaching that appeals to those who struggle with students whose learning styles are not in the mainstream.

Arianna's Story

Arianna Corbuski had an excellent ten-year career in the chemical industry. Married but with no children, she was forced to leave her native Houston for Detroit when her husband got a promotion to a high-level job. Her Houston headquarters had no affiliated office in Detroit.

Arianna didn't want to leave her beloved job or industry, but she also wasn't about to let her husband move well over a thousand miles away without her. She knew she could continue working in her professional area (quality assurance), but she would have to change industry.

She targeted the big industry in Detroit: cars. She knew she had to learn the concepts and language of this new industry, so she worked out a plan of research and networking to develop a job through the hidden job market.

Targeting a New Industry with Confidence

Arianna started simply – checking the Internet for car trade magazines. Reading these helped her learn industry language the insiders used. She then did another search on the General Motors (GM) web page under 'employment' and scrolled down to Quality Assurance (her professional skills area). This fed her lots of good general information that helped her pick up the language inside GM and be prepared to apply it to any car company.

Arianna was already a member of the Institute of Industrial Engineers, and they had a Detroit branch. Six of the local officers were affiliated with the Big Three, so she e-mailed all of them. They referred her to quality issues and papers so she could learn what quality skills were most in demand in the car business. She also joined the Engineering Society of Detroit, where she made new friends who gave her names of their colleagues in the car industry for her to communicate with.

Two CV Formats

Although Arianna focused primarily on the car industry, she kept the door open for other Quality Assurance jobs. She therefore had a chronological CV that had been cleansed of chemical industry language, and also produced a targeted CV very specific to the car industry. The next few pages show the CV formats, followed by a commentary on each.

ARIANNA CORBUSKI

58 Blue Mountain Road
Houston, TX 12345
Residence: (555) 123-4567
Office: (555) 123-7654
ariac@internetprovider.com

OBJECTIVE: QUALITY MANAGEMENT/IMPROVEMENT CONSULTANT

SKILLS SUMMARY:

- Over ten years' experience in quality management/quality assurance
- Skills in assessing and evaluating customer requirements and business objectives
- Develop and deploy organization-wide improvement strategies
- Integrate organizational designs with interlocking natural unit teams
- Match skill-development needs with appropriate level and delivery of training
- Design systems and internal support for continuous improvement
- Implement and follow up consulting to put principles into practice

EXPERIENCE:

1994–present   Canfield Chemical Company (CCC), Houston, TX

2001–2002   Canfield Photo Division Company (CPD), Houston, TX

2002–present   **Quality Management Consultant:**

- Consultant for CCC's Administrative Organization Redesign process and strategic intent initiative.
- Maintained full responsibility for developing and implementing plans/courses of action for several management and technical teams.

2001–2002   **Canfield Photo Quality Core Team Leader:**

- Original member responsible for initiating and leading the CP Quality Leadership Process in two of the largest business units, three major support organizations, and the Latin American region, impacting close to 3,000 employees.
- Developed a network of internal consultants.

1999–2001   **Pilot Team Manager** in Textile Fibres Division:

- Coordinator for entire Team Management effort with full responsibility for seventy interlocking teams.
- As a design team member, pioneered planning, implementing, and coaching facets of the quality process.

1994–1999   **Project Industrial Engineer and Systems Analyst**

- Acted as liaison between two divisions.

EDUCATION: BS in Industrial Engineering/Operations Research, Texas A & M

ADDITIONAL TRAINING:

- Formal Quality Training, Marlboro Institute, Quality Management/Leadership Process
- Team Management Consultant Training
- Performance Management
- Decision-making Styles; Listening Skills
- Deming Philosophy; Statistical Methods; Problem Solving and Group Dynamics

PROFESSIONAL AFFILIATIONS:

- Institute of Industrial Engineers; have served in all officer capacities
- American Society of Quality Control
- Engineering Society of Detroit

ARIANNA CORBUSKI

58 Blue Mountain Road
Houston, TX 12345
Residence: (555) 123-4567
Office: (555) 123-7654
ariac@yahoo.com

TARGETED OBJECTIVE:

QUALITY MANAGEMENT EXECUTIVE: CAR INDUSTRY

CAPABILITIES:

- Assess and evaluate customer requirements and business objectives
- Develop and deploy organization-wide improvement strategies
- Apply Six Sigma to national or international business units as needed
- Design systems and internal support for continuous improvement
- Integrate organizational designs with interlocking natural unit teams
- Implement and follow up consulting to put principles into practice

ACCOMPLISHMENTS:

- Consulted on a major chemical company's administrative organization redesign process and strategic intent initiative that yielded a 22 per cent increase in productivity with a 13 per cent reduction in staff.
- Maintained full responsibility for developing and implementing plans and courses of action for six management teams and 23 technical teams for four divisions.
- Originated and led the Quality Leadership Process in two large business units (over 1,000 each), three major support organizations, and the Latin American region, impacting close to 3,000 employees.
- Developed a cost-saving infrastructure of dynamic internal consultants through training and strategic advising.
- Coordinated team management effort with full responsibility for seventy interlocking teams. Pioneered planning, implementing, and coaching facets of the quality process.

WORK HISTORY:

1994–present   CANFIELD CHEMICAL COMPANY Houston, TX

2001–2002   CANFIELD PHOTO COMPANY Houston, TX

2002–present	**Quality Management Consultant**
2001–2002	**Canfield Photo Quality Core Team Leader**
1999–2001	**Pilot Team Manager**
1994–1999	**Project Industrial Engineer; Systems Analyst**

EDUCATION: BS in Industrial Engineering/Operations Research, Texas A & M

ADDITIONAL TRAINING:

* Six Sigma Black Belt
* Quality Training, Marlboro Institute
* Quality Management/Leadership Process
* Team Management; Performance Management
* Decision-making Styles
* Listening skills
* Deming philosophy
* Statistical Methods
* Problem Solving and Group Dynamics

PROFESSIONAL AFFILIATIONS:

Institute of Industrial Engineers; have served in all officer capacities

American Society of Quality Control

Engineering Society of Detroit

Commentary on Arianna's Choices

1. **Objective** She's stating the obvious. She could leave this off, but as it is the first thing scanned, it will help.

2. **Skills Summary** This is a straightforward list of skills including the all-important nouns that must be in the summary to be effective for scanning.

3. **Experience/chronological history** Most notable here is that Arianna wrote her title in bold and left her company name in plain text. She's selling the titles over the company name. She could go back further than ten years, but her work history at this one company is sufficient to demonstrate her professional growth.

4. **Education, supporting data, and professional affiliations** She left out the date of her graduation (not necessary). With a two-page CV, it's always best to have most of the work history on the first page and all supporting data on the second.

Targeted CV

1. **Targeted Objective** With the targeted format you must be absolutely specific to the job title.

2. **Capabilities** Most of Arianna's capabilities are taken from her skills summary. Therefore she doesn't need a summary using this format.

3. **Accomplishments** Here she disconnected her accomplishments from the specific titles. This allows Arianna to be more selective in favour of the aspects of her achievements most likely to appeal to the car industry. She does, however, mention in her covering letter that she would be happy to send the chronological CV as well if requested.

4. **Work History** The bare-bones list of where and when. The 'What' is up in the accomplishments section.

5. **Education, etc.** As in her chronological CV, all the supporting data is best left on the second page, as long as the first page is already filled with relevant history, skills, and achievements.

Cornell French's Story

DEALING UP FRONT WITH POST-TRAUMATIC STRESS DISORDER

Cornell French served in the Gulf War. He distinguished himself there and throughout his later military career over the next twelve years. As platoon leader in the 1991 war, Cornell was taking his group into battle, and in a tragic 'friendly fire' accident, he witnessed the deaths of five young soldiers under his command. He was sent to the hospital to recover from shock and temporarily reassigned from battle. However, his recovery was swift, and he was back at his former assignment within two weeks.

Leaving the Marine Corps, he enrolled at university and gained a master's degree. Armed with an advanced degree from a prestigious university, he was about to make the transition from military to civilian work. But the transition was just one part of his challenge.

Unhealed Wounds Re-emerge

With the help of a career adviser Cornell had written a good CV; however, his interviews were disasters. Every time he was asked about his Gulf War experiences, he would clam up. With every succeeding question about anything related to his skills or even his recent studies, he seemed to lose confidence and acted as though he was hiding something.

His memories of the traumatic event, reawakened by the tragic death of his brother the past summer, led to post-traumatic stress disorder, and he couldn't deal with any memory of or questions about the Gulf War. With encouragement he finally got the therapy he deserved and medication to reduce his anxiety.

A Double Strategy

Cornell discovered a way to ask his interviewers to avoid the subject of the Gulf War. He would say, 'I'd prefer not to discuss my time in the Gulf War. Although my leadership there was commended, the details of war are unsavoury.'

Then, at the suggestion of his counsellor, he sought and received a commendation letter from his commanding officer at the time, one that underscored his skills and bravery. When he was close to a job offer, he told the interviewer, 'I have a commendation letter I want you to see from my commanding officer during the first Gulf War explaining an incident that left me with a treatable condition that might require some accommodation on this job.'

CORNELL FRENCH III

16 Broadlane Avenue #24
Cambridge, MA 12345
(555) 123-4567
cfrench@internetprovider.net

OBJECTIVE: International Diplomacy – Any Country

EDUCATION

- The Harvard School of Law and Diplomacy, Harvard University
- Master of Arts in International Relations, May 2005
- Ames College, Dover, Del. B.A. May 1992.
- Nominated for Harry S Truman National Scholarship

INTERNATIONAL EXPERIENCE

- Travelled extensively: 49 states, The Netherlands, Italy, Okinawa, Republic of the Philippines, Republic of Korea, People's Republic of China, Hong Kong, Cairo, Dubai, Iraq, and Kuwait.
- Working knowledge of Portuguese and Russian.

PROFESSIONAL EXPERIENCE

- Research Assistant, Harvard Law School, 2003–2005
- Liaison Officer, 1st Battalion, 1st Marines, Camp Pendleton, 2000–2003
- Surveillance and Target Acquisition Platoon Commander, 1991–2000
- Executive Officer/Platoon Commander, Bravo Company, 1990–1991

SKILLS SUMMARY

Leadership / Training / Programme Development

- Chief Instructor for Squad Leader courses; developed a comprehensive programme of instruction and field training to teach leadership under extreme stress.
- Coordinated the actions of 40 students, 8 instructors, and 45 support personnel.
- Chosen to screen, select, and train 45 qualified Marines for elite reconnaissance and target-acquisition missions.
- Conducted prep training using digital video that twice produced the top two graduates of the Marine Corps' most demanding special school.

CORNELL FRENCH III   (555) 123-4567   french@internetprovider.net

- Developed comprehensive training in land navigation, communications, and patrolling culminating in a week of unprecedented independent operations in the Mojave Desert.
- Co-developed original doctrine for cliff assaults, later adopted throughout the Marine Corps.

Organizational Management

- Coordinated the training schedules of a battalion's six subordinate companies. Scheduled and coordinated all training for the Marine Corps' first fully qualified raid force throughout a six-month deployment to the Persian Gulf.
- As Officer-in-Charge of a US Marine Mobile Training Team, supervised weapons and tactics training of 300 Philippine Marines, Republic of the Philippines.

Research/Analysis/Writing/Editing

- Master's theses: *Vietnam: Reporters and the My Lai Crisis of 1968; Rethinking and Reinforcement in NATO "After the Pact": U.S. Strategies and the Atlantic Alliance.*
- As Historical Officer, researched and wrote an account of a battalion's training and deployment.
- Selected for year-long Honours programme, Department of History, Ames College; thesis: *America in Vietnam 1945–1950: The Origins of an Incomplete War.*
- Delegate to Naval Academy Foreign Affairs Conference, 2000.

INTERESTS

- Active in Representative Assembly, African-American Society, and the Colloquium on Nuclear Weapons and Arms Control, Ames College.

COMMENDATION LETTER

Excerpt from commanding officer's letter:

I have known Cornell French over his entire Marine Corps career. He has admirably served his country in all corners of the world throughout that time.

One of the single most painful and difficult outcomes of war is accidental death. It is public knowledge that some Americans have died from friendly fire: Americans accidentally killing fellow Americans thinking they were the enemy.

During the short days of the ground war in Iraq in 1991, Platoon Commander French and five members of his Bravo Company encountered such friendly fire. All five with him that day were killed. Commander French unfortunately and incorrectly concluded that if only he had led them elsewhere, they would all have survived the Gulf War, as did he. This is sometimes called survivor's guilt. In the case of a platoon commander, this kind of guilt is compounded.

As we routinely do for our officers and soldiers, we sent Cornell to be treated for the overwhelmingly stressful aftermath. He recovered quickly and fully and went back to the Gulf within two weeks to help in the clean-up effort when the war ended.

He then went on to achieve a great deal over his remaining years in the Corps. I believe his CV outlines an outstanding list of accomplishments. It's no surprise to me that he wants to ultimately go into public service. Political research and consulting in any area of international diplomacy is the right step on his career path.

There has been much written and said about Post-traumatic Stress Disorder. Soldiers have long been known to suffer from PTSD. It sometimes doesn't show up until years later when a triggering event occurs. Cornell recently suffered a tragedy in his family that reawakened PTSD. His current treatment is going well, I understand.

Sometimes accommodations are necessary for this condition, and sometimes they are not. I assume if you have been given this commendation you are sufficiently interested in Commander French that you will be discussing this yourselves. Suffice it to say, he is an accomplished, gifted, and thoroughly responsible man who through no fault of his own suffered from the toils of war. This in no way should impact his career, provided the conditions are appropriate.

Feel free to contact me if you have any further questions.

Commentary on Cornell's Choices

1. **Objective** This was Cornell's first draft before he began information interviewing (networking). He named a category, but no specific title since his skills could cover a number of jobs in the field of diplomacy. When he got into further interviews, he changed the objective to fit the job description.

2. **Education** Although Cornell is already in his thirties and has had thirteen years of work experience, his master's degree is very recent, so education goes at the top of the CV. If you graduated four or more years ago, put the education category at the end of the CV.

3. **International Experience/Professional Experience** Cornell put his international experience first and into a separate category for special emphasis, since he wants international diplomatic work. His work history is primarily military, so he must account for titles, dates, and places.

4. **Skills/Accomplishments Summary** Cornell put all his skills and accomplishments under focused functional categories. He started with leadership and training, since these are most pertinent to his job target. They are not the most recent skills he has been using, since he has spent the past two years at university. The functional CV allows him to flag older skills before presenting more recent skills that reflect only his education, but no direct experience.

Commendation Letter

1. **Introduction** The commanding officer establishes his relationship with Cornell and immediately praises him for his years of service.

2. *The entire story* is carefully told. It is made clear to the reader that what happened to the young platoon commander was a tragic accident completely out of his control, but that it left its scars, nonetheless.

3. *The remainder of his military career* is praised as well as his recent studies. This is where the commanding officer is fully endorsing Cornell's capability as well as his new career choice.

4. Finally, *the most delicate issue is abstractly outlined*: accommodations to ensure his well-being on the job and the support needed for him to deliver to the best of his capability. Cornell is praised again for his overall military career and his personal character.

The Story of Two Women Going for One Job

Marilyn earned her BA in economics, married her childhood sweetheart, and worked in banking for five years before taking time off to raise two young children. Marilyn's fellow Parent Teacher Association (PTA) member Donna, also a mother of school-age children, was recently divorced and finishing up her degree in horticulture.

Already generous volunteers, both of the women now longed for paid half-time work.

Marilyn sought out a career counsellor, who took her through a series of steps to get to what made her 'sizzle': landscape gardening. Marilyn's parents had always owned a gardening business; this intense kind of work never caught her attention as a possible career choice until she visited home during summer breaks from college. Unfortunately, by the time she graduated they had closed the business, and she moved on to marriage and into corporate life. However, when she checked with the counsellor, landscape gardening came through as a strong recommendation.

The Next Opportunity May Be Very Close to Home

Marilyn and Donna met while serving on the same PTA committee to beautify the school grounds. One day the conversation led to their mutual interest in landscape gardening, organic gardening, and horticulture, as well as their mutual job needs.

Neither considered herself an 'entrepreneur'. Neither needed to earn a big salary. Donna's divorce settlement was generous enough to allow her to spend half her time with her children. This was not fundamentally different from Marilyn's sharing her husband's income and parenting.

Making One Small Business Idea Work for Two Without Overwhelming Either

Marilyn and Donna decided to make their combined skills add up to one reliable, desirable entity. They created a CV of their combined talents packaged as subcontractors to a small or medium-sized landscape business.

They addressed some anticipated objections to their combined CV in their covering letter. This is a smart move: it lets any potential employer/contractor know the parameters of their flexible time. It offers a realistic assessment of service and value without blind expectations (which can lead to frustration and disappointment).

MARILYN KADINSKI
22 Parkland View Road
Armonk, NY 12456
555-123-7654

DONNA M. LORELLI
154 Huett Place
W. Armonk, NY 12456
555-123-4567

mardon@internetprovider.com

3 April, 2005

Mr. Geoffrey Beaucuse
Perennial Gardens of Greenwich
123 Langley Lane
Greenwich, CT 12345

Dear Mr. Beaucuse,

It was a pleasure meeting you on Saturday at the Silent Auction. The PTA raised over $60,000 for the evening. My partner Donna and I have recently set up a subcontracting business, and we were both drawn to your generous offering at the Silent Table: the photos of your work were exquisite and align perfectly with our own organic philosophy and artistic skills.

We believe that as on-site managers or gardeners we can offer your company a combined skill base and flexible time schedule that will prove that two heads *and able bodies* are better than one.

- Firstly, job sharing allows us to double our value to your company through our combined skills of horticulture education, hands-on experience, a wider network of potential clients, and a larger pool of information.

- Secondly, our dual passion for the earth is acknowledged through our absolute dedication to the use of organic methods of gardening, creating naturalized outdoor environments that meet today's needs for global environmental awareness.

- Thirdly, job sharing allows each of us to be energetic in a highly physical job. We will have virtually no absences as each of us can easily cover for the other when needed.

You indicated that your business is growing and you expect this summer to be very busy, so I'd like to show you some photos of our work. Perhaps Donna and I can take on some of your new business as subcontractors. I'll phone you in a few days to see when you might have some time for a brief visit.

Sincerely,

Marilyn Kadinski

MARILYN KADINSKI
22 Parkland View Road
Armonk, NY 12456
555-123-7654

DONNA M. LORELLI
154 Huett Place
W. Armonk, NY 12456
555-123-4567

mardon@internetprovider.com

SUBCONTRACTORS: Assistant Gardener/On-site Manager, Bringing Beauty, Biodiversity, and Environmental Integrity to Local Medium-sized Landscape Company.

Capabilities:

- Complete knowledge of non-toxic alternative herbicide and pesticide methods.
- Prepare and implement seasonal garden plan; watering, weeding, fertilizing, pruning, deadheading, mulching, using manure strategically.
- Knowledge of soil and regional soil conditions.
- Design organic, zone-friendly shade gardens, drought/deer-resistant gardens for home owner or business.
- Manage small staff.
- Install small- to large-scale organic gardens.
- Maintain garden installations.
- Operational on equipment: backhoe, lawn mowers, blowers, and power shears.
- Informed and knowledgeable about yardage when ordering soils and mulches.
- Ability to engage in hard physical labour; able to lift up to 50 pounds.

Achievements

- Assisted and successfully communicated in Spanish, with a team of three Salvadoran landscapers on four medium-sized, successful, commercial installations all completed within the same month for M&T Bank offices.
- Studied the effects of pH-matching for highly acidic-soil to near neutral-soil plants.
- Developed a container growing system to help plants develop before planting in mismatched soil.
- Implemented a drip irrigation system that kept large estate gardens thriving and water bills lowered during drought.
- Selected and installed deer-resistant perennial shade garden utilizing a combination of nursery-grown native plants for client on limited budget.

Credentials and Education: 1989 to the present:

Six years in hands-on work with family-owned gardening business
AA degree in Horticulture and Landscaping, Westchester Community College
BA in business administration, Hofstra University
Combined fifteen-plus years direct experience in organic gardening

Commentary on Marilyn's Choices

Covering Letter

Marilyn and Donna got lucky. Right after they put together their CV and business concept, they happened upon a potential employer, struck up a brief conversation, and followed up immediately.

1. **Opening paragraph** Marilyn opens with a mutual win – her contact volunteered his services for the auction, and the auction was a big success. She has the perfect opportunity to praise her contact, having recently seen pictures of his work.

2. **Middle paragraph** She jumps right into her sales pitch. With each bulleted comment she drives home a different selling point showing how the two women have a combined value far greater than one person can usually offer.

3. **Closing paragraph** Again, Marilyn wastes no time. She assumes there might be a need for their subcontracting services since she already knows her contact is going to be inundated with upcoming work. She asks to show their photos (these are pictures of their own personal gardens since they're just starting out and don't yet have a client list), and she forecasts her phone call.

Two-person CV

1. **Title** They use very specific descriptors of what their subcontracting vision is and who their targeted employers would be.

2. **Capabilities** They cover every possibility that would appeal to any landscaping firm. They know and address the needs of the local customers and are particularly aware of the many customers in their area who want *only* organic gardening.

3. **Achievements** Purposefully selective, they nonetheless demonstrate a broad range of past accomplishments, including commercial installations, estate gardens, limited budget gardening, and inventive problem solving.

4. **Credentials and Education** There are no specific dates attached to their education and credentials, only the summary dates, 1989 to the present. They don't want to highlight how long ago Marilyn worked in her family business.

Another choice both women could make is to assume a business name, with a business card, flyers, and other advertising tactics. They kept it simpler starting out as they wished to land steady work with one medium-sized landscaper so they could enhance their current skills before they became independent and moved into freelance work.

PART SIX

Perfect CVs

O n the following pages are forty CVs, two of which have accompanying covering letters. All but eight of the CVs are formatted to one page.

The CVs are organized by level: Entry (pages 179 to 190), Mid-level, (pages 191 to 203), and Senior (pages 204 to 223).

• In most cases the entry-level CVs are by new college graduates looking for their first jobs after graduation.

• The mid-level CVs are from people who've been working for at least five years. Some have no degrees and some have advanced degrees.

• The senior CVs are mostly by executives or professionals, usually with long work histories. More than half of the two-page CVs are senior level. Several of the senior CVs are for freelance or consulting work.

There are many industries included, as well as all four CV formats. On each CV page is a comment letting you know why this format is best or what feature to look at specifically in this CV.

These CVs are based on those of real people. They have been revised and disguised to protect the identities of the people whose CVs became part of this project. Every CV was selected to teach you, the reader, how to organize your data in a clear and attractive way. If you see inconsistencies, it's because each CV was written by and for a distinct personality. Every CV has a structure, but what was added or taken away was always done with a purpose: to get the interview! This is also true of the covering letters.

Feel free to copy aspects of any CV that would enhance your own (as long as it's also appropriate for you). But beware of looking for a CV that fits you so closely that you can lift it right from the book. In fact, no two people have the same skills and accomplishments in the same industry, executed exactly the same way and at the same time. These CVs should therefore only be used as a guide. Your own CV should be tailored to reflect your unique talents and experiences and customized with your individual Job Targets in mind.

On the next page is a CV review index to help you find the CVs closest to your own needs.

Industry/Job Target Or Title	Chronological	Functional	Targeted	Resume Alternative	Covering Letter	Professional Level	Pg
Health/Spa Manager	✓					M	196
Health/Operations Supervisor	✓					M	198
Health/Public Relations		✓				E	186
Health/Sports Medicine Therapist		✓				E	184
Health/Medical Research				✓		E	188
IT/Systems Analyst	✓					M	200
IT/Circuit Designer			✓			M	204
Financial/Accounting Auditor	✓					E	187
Financial/Banking Management	✓					S	220
Financial/Banking Operations Analyst	✓					S	208
Philanthropy	✓					S	212
Employment Facilitator			✓			M	195
Employment/Personnel Interviewer				✓		E	189
Employment/Career Counsellor	✓				✓	M	138
Chemical/Quality Assurance	✓		✓			S	156
Chemical/Mining/Chemical Purchasing	✓					S	213
Materials Science Consultant	✓					S	210
Materials Science/HAZMATS Consultant		✓				S	216
Architecture/Architect			✓			M	197
Business/Marketing		✓				E	180
Education/Professor			✓		✓	M	148
Landscaping Consultant(s)			✓		✓	E	169
Journalism/Reporter		✓				M	203
Newspapers/Editor	✓				✓	S	218
Publishing/Staff Writer			✓			E	183
Telecom Consultant			✓			M	207
Telecom/Conference Manager			✓			M	199
Hospitality/Travel/Events			✓			E	181

Industry/Job Target Or Title	Chronological	Functional	Targeted	Resume Alternative	Covering Letter	Professional Level	Pg
Food/Restaurant/Caterer	✓					M	223
Fashion/Buyer's Assistant		✓				M	205
Legal/Lawyer		✓				S	217
Design/Graphic Artist		✓				M	193
Packaging/Secretary	✓					M	194
Insurance/Legal Supervisor		✓				S	215
Engineering/Main Tech		✓				M	202
Urban Planning/Research		✓				E	185
Social Service/Research			✓			E	182
Public Service/Diplomacy		✓				M	161
Software/Sales	✓					S	214
Energy/International Sales	✓					S	222
Engineer/Industrial	✓					M	221
Proofreading	✓				✓	M	191

Comments: Franklyn is late in the race to approach this company. The traditional recruiting season is over; however, he wants an interview and is willing to stick his neck out and ask for an informal interview anyway. His letter shows he has done his homework on this company (this is a must).

FRANKLYN STEWART GRAVES
2213 Harbor Side
Lubbock, TX 12345
(555) 234-5678
graves@internetprovider.net

2 June, 2004

Mr. Sheldon P. Hoffman
Assistant Director, Marketing, Sales Solutions
Texas Instruments Corporation
123 Fair Boulevard
Dallas, TX 12345

Dear Mr. Hoffman,

I had the privilege of attending your Infocomm Conference in San Diego last summer. I was in awe at your presentation of the Digital Light Processing story. I've followed TI in the press for the past year and watched your growth in the stock market. TI is impressive; it must be very competitive for new graduates to enter your workforce.

However, I love competition. It's what good business is built on, and it's what any successful new recruit must thrive on. I had interviews in March with over a dozen good companies during our Spring Job Fair at Hamden University and have subsequently received several respectable offers, but unfortunately these would all require me to stay on the East Coast. I've managed to put a few offers on hold, since I wanted to pursue employment at TI this summer when I'm back in my home state.

My CV will show you a broad range of skills and, most importantly, leadership qualities. Hamden is a military college and is known for instilling rigorous discipline of mind and behaviour. I am proud of my college success and want to start a career in marketing where I can prove myself with the kind of company that leads the industry in its innovative products and quality customer service.

I have 'studied' Texas Instruments as if it were a course, without an examination. I want the opportunity to take the examination now. I am available to travel up to Dallas at any time within the next three weeks. I would be honoured to have thirty minutes with you to explore the marketing of TI products. I realize it may be too late for the new recruit season, but I also know I can wait, even if I start with another company, which I will have to begin to do soon. I'll phone you in a few days. I hope we meet in person.

Respectfully,

Franklyn Stewart Graves

Comments: Franklyn's CV highlights excellent course work and training, as well as college achievements. His marketing work experience is also a plus for him, and military leadership can be coveted in the business world.

FRANKLYN STEWART GRAVES

Campus Address: Hamden University, 123 North Dr., Hamden, CT. 12345 Phone: (555)-232-0000
Permanent Address: 2213 Harbor Side, Lubbock TX, 67891 Phone: (555)-779-0000
graves@internetprovider.net

JOB TARGET: ENTRY LEVEL IN BUSINESS MARKETING

EDUCATION

HAMDEN UNIVERSITY, MILITARY COLLEGE OF CONNECTICUT	Hamden, CT
BS in Psychology, Minor in Business Marketing	May 2004
Dean's List, 3 Consecutive Semesters	

COURSE WORK RELEVANT TO MARKETING AND BUSINESS

Advertising	International Business	Social Psychology
Marketing Management	Introduction to Business	Military
Small Business Strategies	Mass Media	Leadership Lab I, II, III

Psychology Senior Research: Positive and Negative Framing in Advertising

SKILLS

Computer MS Excel, Word, PowerPoint, and Adobe Workshop
Languages Conversational Spanish
Other Supervisory and leadership skills developed in Corps of Cadets

MARKETING EXPERIENCE

FINISHING TOUCHES	Lubbock, TX	2002–present
Marketing and Sales Consultant for Start-up Company		Summer & part time

Head of Marketing Development

- Developed portfolio of primary pieces of work for presentation to potential clients
- Developed marketing plan to enhance business relationships
- Set up strategy meetings with local entrepreneur to increase sales
- Sold services of company to target market statewide

OTHER WORK EXPERIENCE

GOLD'S GYM	Lubbock, TX	
• *Weight Room Coordinator*		2001 Summer
SPECIALTY CONCRETE / GRAY DOVES DESIGN	Lubbock, TX	
• *Concrete and Landscape Staff Member*		1998–2000 Summer

ACTIVITIES AND LEADERSHIP

- **Corps of Cadets** Hamden University is a private military college instilling leadership, integrity, discipline, and moral development.
- **Duty Corporal** Carry out assigned duties such as Security, Flag Ceremony, and President Escort
- **SSG Cadre** Train new recruits of Military Police Company to be upper-class cadets
- **1st Lt. Executive Officer** Second in command of Military Police Company, comprising of 18 cadets – assign duties to cadets, supervise cadets to ensure job completion, prepare cadet evaluations
- **Football** Team member first year

Comments: Marietta's targeted CV is aimed at one specific employer. She also wanted to de-emphasize her multiple, unrelated jobs.

MARIETTA MULVEY
155 Pine Road
New Paltz, NY 12345
555-123-4567
mulvey@internetprovider.net

JOB TARGET:

- THEME WEEK EVENTS PLANNER — Mohonk Mountain House

CAPABILITIES:

- Organize seasonal activities from skiing to competitive skating to botanical healing plants to summer gardening tours for visiting groups.
- Write activities schedules for multiple groups, from children to teens to older people.
- Develop programmes for women's health, including yoga and diet instruction.
- Create, invent, and implement concepts and all activities for specialty theme weeks.
- Delegate all aspects of theme weeks; oversee execution and control budgets.
- Implement creative plans to hands-on decorating and to execute thematic details for hotel/resort venues.

ACHIEVEMENTS:

- Organized New York University's Annual Alumni Day activities: 1,500 alums.
- Managed, planned, and coordinated special catering events, including the opening of the Mellon Wing at the National Gallery, which hosted 150 guests.
- Developed a Middle Ages spring festival with over 50 vendors and performers visited by approximately 1,500 guests over three-day period.
- Managed popular Brooklyn Heights, NY, restaurant and catering establishment.
- Provided educational programmes in museums, theatres, and botanical gardens.
- Scheduled and coordinated various aspects involved in successful production of parties, special events, performances, and festivals.
- Designed decoration materials for culinary exhibition, including floral and food.

WORK HISTORY:

2002–present	Senior Research Clerk, New York University, New York, NY
1997–present	Assistant to Director/Executive Board Medieval Arts Council, New York, NY
1996–1997	Teacher — 3rd Grade, PS 141, New York Board of Education, New York, NY
1992–1994	Sous Chef — Assistant Manager — Part-time Caterer
	La Petite Coq, Brooklyn Heights, NY

EDUCATION:

2003	Columbia University — MS, Education
2000	Barnard College BS Graduate Programme — Medieval History
1992	Marjorie Farmer's Modern Gourmet Cooking School — Chef's Diploma

Comments: Mary Lynn left college a year ago and is disappointed with the kind of business her legal firm handles. She chooses the targeted format to focus on her capability in a new career direction.

MARY LYNN PALARMO
12322 Sepulveda Boulevard
Los Angeles, CA 12345
(555) 123-4567
palarmo@internetprovider.net

OBJECTIVE: Research Assistant for an Organization Addressing Social Welfare Issues

EDUCATION: BA SYRACUSE UNIVERSITY Pre-law and Urban Studies 2003
Certified Paralegal, National Paralegal Association

CAPABILITIES:

- Write complete and detailed research reports.
- Edit written materials for content and grammar.
- Work well under pressure to meet deadlines.
- Communicate effectively with librarians and staff required to support research work.
- Skilled in the use of Internet research tools: AltaVista Advanced Query, Electronic Law Resources, and Google Usenet.
- Read and provide executive summaries of detailed material.
- Prepare charts and visual materials using both Windows and Mac.

ACHIEVEMENTS:

- Wrote a research report on the effect of crowding and reported incidences of violence; results used by non-profit organization in grant application for additional funding.
- Developed a system to track prices of common purchases to assist non-profit organization with limited funding to serve more clients.
- Researched background material for textbook on urban issues by Professor Louis Hornbeck.
- Edited university political magazine and wrote more than a dozen articles on pertinent and controversial social issues.
- Retrieved cases and briefs and checked citations related to current lawsuits.
- Analysed data using statistical programs SPSS and SAS.
- Conducted research project on levels of moral development on group decision making.

EMPLOYMENT HISTORY:

2003–2004   PARALEGAL
Law Offices of Moore and Wallace, Los Angeles, CA
Specialist in Corporate Fraud and Corporate Bankruptcy

Summers
2000–2003   NANNY for family travelling to South of France for 90-day stays.
Visited nine additional countries, many villages, museums, and student hostels. Developed conversational French and can read Italian.

Comments: Lewis chose a targeted format, as his objective is absolutely specific. He has lots of good experience to show in his capabilities and achievements sections. Note how he includes self-study, which enhances course work.

LEWIS LEVINE

Levine@internetprovider.com

College: 123 Soverill Road
Norfolk, VA 12345
555-123-4567

12 Country Life Estates
Ladue, MO 12345
555-123-7654

EDUCATION: BA, Old Dominion University, Norfolk, VA
Subjects: Journalism, Biology. Graduation: May 2004

JOB TARGET: Staff Writer for Major Land Grant University Publications Dept

COURSE STUDY AND SELF-STUDY:

Science & the Industrial Classes   Applying Jeffersonian Ideals
The Homestead Act   History of People's Colleges
The Land-Grant Act of 1890   US Tribal College History

CAPABILITIES:

- Write clear, concise proposals to meet goals within tight deadlines.
- Research topics using Internet search engines or print resources.
- Interview experts to obtain current information for timely reporting.
- Know marketing strategies; write copy to attract readers, promote services.
- Work with team members to produce a comprehensive, balanced view of multi-faceted topics.
- Produce copy to communicate ideas clearly to customers of diverse educational backgrounds; explain complex topics in a straightforward way.
- Itemize required outcomes based on past performance and future goals.

ACHIEVEMENTS:

- Researched multiple topics related to how scientific research affects our daily lives.
- Interviewed local dignitaries for a four-part article on the environmental impact of a controversial new master plan.
- Created and wrote a weekly column on current 'hot' topics for paper circulated to 2,500 undergraduate students; column quoted in local city paper.
- Trained new staff in interviewing techniques, ways to condense information to create interesting, readable copy.
- Covered periodic board and committee meetings, submitting articles on topics of interest to readership.

WORK HISTORY:

2001–2004   *Old Dominion Ledger*, Norfolk, VA: Junior Copy Writer
1998–2001   *St. Louis Courier*, Chesterfield, MO: Staff 'Cub' Writer

Comments: Nicholas's CV format is functional, since his job during all four summers of college was unrelated to his future work. With a degree in physiotherapy, he wants to focus on sports injuries. He has his own sports background to add as a valuable featured category.

NICHOLAS KOSTASTANZ
43 Greavey Road
Terre Haute, IN 12345
555-123-4567
555-321-7654 (cell)
kostastanz@internetprovider.net

JOB TARGET: PHYSIOTHERAPIST – SPORTS MEDICINE

EDUCATION:

BS in Physiotherapy, Indiana State University, Gary, IN, May 2004

CAPABILITIES:

- Understand a variety of sports-related injuries from personal experience.
- Knowledge and skill to use electrical stimulation, hot packs, cold compresses, and ultrasound to relieve pain and reduce swelling.
- Provide empathy, focus, and commitment to increase flexibility and range of motion.
- Improve patients' strength, balance, coordination, and endurance.

SPORTS ACCOMPLISHMENTS:

- Played halfback in college team for two years.
- Won silver medal on competitive swim team 2002, 2004.
- Ran a Saturday tennis clinic 2003–2004 with maximum class attendance.

PHYSICAL THERAPY TRAINING:

- Trained in:
  —cardiopulmonary and neurological rehabilitation
  —physiotherapy measurement and assessment
  —electrotherapy and electrophysiological testing
- Orthopaedics and medical/surgical rehabilitation
- Medical/surgical pathophysiology

EXPERIENCE and AWARDS:

2000–2003   Four years of summers as a trainee with the Terre Haute Rescue Squad, working with emergency victims under guidance of chief squad leader.

Six months as a trainee, St. Mary's Rehabilitation Clinic, observing senior physiotherapist working with a variety of injuries and age groups.

Camp counsellor, YMCA Camp Kahikatoa, supervising children aged 8–13, assisting camp nurse with minor injuries.

Qualified in the top 15 per cent of physiotherapy graduates in 2004 class for licensure.

Comments: Jorge's work as a trainee comes off better in the functional format, since his most recent experience is unrelated to his objective.

JORGE GARCIA

University of Montana
Ramson Hall, Rm.27
1001 North Gate Lane
Missoula, Montana 12453
555-123-4567

5453 Bright Light Blvd.
Las Vegas, NV 12345
555-312-4657

jorgec@internetprovider.net

OBJECTIVE: Research Assistant, Greater Las Vegas Urban Planning

EDUCATION:

BS Urban Planning, University of Montana, Missoula,
Graduation expected May 2004

URBAN PLANNING:

Wrote detailed analyses of traffic congestion and projected commercial impact of three shopping developments on West End.

Utilized analytical technique to project costs of suburban impact from shopping development sprawl.

Researched, wrote, and delivered white paper on zoning and code issues as well as environmental impact of shopping development number 1.

RESEARCH:

Developed prototype of affordable housing model allowing suitable compromise for nearby wetlands.

Studied and wrote thesis on commercial expansion in suburban communities and effects on employment picture.

Attended numerous town meetings and developed back-up facts/data for urban planning professional.

WORK EXPERIENCE:

2002–03, Summers	Office Assistant at Garcia Construction
2001	Rock Canyon Development Corp. Las Vegas, NV. Trainee, research on developing water rights for new suburban development in Red Rock Canyon area of Las Vegas.
1998–2000, Summers	Garcia Construction, Las Vegas, NV. Labourer

Comments: Sonya has a good degree, but doesn't need to flag it as she has other good experience to start in her field. Her fluency in Chinese is a big plus, particularly since she wants to return to her home town of San Francisco.

SONYA LEHANI CHU

University of Colorado
Compton Hall, Rm. 27
111 University Lane
Boulder, CO 12345
(555) 321-7654

456 Sunflower Street
San Leandro, CA 21345
(555) 123-4567

chu@internetprovider.com

JOB TARGET: Public Affairs/Public Relations, Health Care

EDUCATION:

BA in Public Relations, University of Colorado at Boulder
Emphasis in Public Affairs Writing, 2004 graduation expected

Course Work Included

Corporate Public Relations	Interaction with the Media
Public Relations Writing	Crisis Management
Public Speaking I and II	Reporting for Public Affairs
Publication Design	Writing for Broadcasting

PUBLIC RELATIONS EXPERIENCE:

Co-created pre-operative question-and-answer material used by Hospital Public Relations Representative for families with children entering Holy Cross Hospital for routine surgery.

Organized mock informational workshops on new pharmaceuticals between chemistry and medicine students at University of Colorado.

Self-published monthly newsletter on dorm life during stay at Compton Hall dormitory, producing 225 copies a month for a two-year period.

OTHER WORK:

Summer 2001–2004
Sales, Radio Shack, Pleasant Hills Mall, San Leandro, CA

Summer 2001
Chamber of Commerce, San Leandro, CA
Attendant at information booth, assisting visitors on locating activities, lodging, and restaurants in and around the Bay Area region.
Trainee: Our Redeemer Hospital Customer Relations Dept.

ACTIVITIES AND INTERESTS:

Volunteer in Literacy for America teaching reading to adolescents.

Speak fluent Chinese; taught English to Chinese immigrants.

Comments: Sarah's trainee work and summer jobs show the same skills as her specialization and her job objective. The chronological format works in her favour.

CHRONOLOGICAL CV

Sarah Featherstone

Campus:
879 Vanderlyn Hall
Philadelphia, PA 12345
555-123-4567 (cell)

Permanent:
123 Kortrey Street
Gainesville, FL 21345
555-321-5674

featherstone@internetprovider.com

OBJECTIVE: Public Accounting Auditor in the Greater Pittsburgh Area

SUMMARY:
- Two years of progressive accounting and auditing
- Auditor trainee with Deloitte and Touche in New York City
- Proficient with MS Office, Windows XP, and the Internet

EDUCATION: Bachelor of Business Administration in Accounting, expected May 2004
University of Philadelphia, Philadelphia, PA

Managerial Accounting	Corporate Audit and Reconciliation
Intermediate Accounting I & II	Financial Management
Accounting I & II	Internal Audit
Accounting for Not-for-profits	Managerial Economics

EXPERIENCE: Auditor Trainee, May 2003 to August 2003
Deloitte and Touche, New York, NY
- Participated in the annual audit of Carrigan Holdings, including development of the final certification report.
- Participated in quarterly audit of Solomon Bank Corporation, including identification and correction of over thirty major accounting errors.
- Developed several Excel spreadsheet macros currently in use for reducing entry time and automatically cross-referencing for errors.

Accounts Payable/Bookkeeping Clerk, May 2003 to August 2003
Gainesville Tax and Bookkeeping Service, Gainesville, FL
- Assisted (via remote) with payroll, tax, and account processing.
- Developed automated monthly sales tax payment system.
- Implemented Rapid Tax Refund service for individual customers.

LEADERSHIP:
- Vice President, Student Accounting Chapter, 2003-2004
- Treasurer, Phi Gamma Alpha Honors Society, 2003-2004
- Resident Assistant, Maxwell Hall 2002-2004

Comments: Veronica's work history has been entirely connected with her studies, but her recent specific assignments speak perfectly to the possible opening with her contact. She makes a compelling case for an interview: she's done similar work and she's writing a thesis on the subject.

Veronica Szerbowski
8443 Londonderry Court
Ann Arbor, MI 12345
555-123-4567
VS@internetprovider.com

Mr. Salvatore Primiano   18 June, 2004
Crescent Medical Consultants
544 Crystalline Road
Ann Arbor, MI 12345

Dear Mr. Primiano,

Dr. Joseph Millian at Michigan's medical school suggested I contact you concerning your work in utilizing innovative administrative methods to keep the frail elderly out of nursing homes and in their own homes as long as possible. He also mentioned you might be considering taking on additional staff to coordinate field investigations as a key component in your study.

Last August I relocated to Ann Arbor to complete my master's degree in social services. I was formerly studying at the University of Nebraska at Lincoln. During my five years as an undergraduate and then graduate there, I headed the Student Social Action Committee, which developed outreach programmes for the elderly in two counties surrounding the Lincoln campus. Our major focus was to get our clients to follow an appropriate regimen for their medications. Our secondary focus was to provide transport and other household services and spread the work among thirty-five volunteers. All of our work was carefully documented and I am currently writing a master's thesis on social action as curriculum for social service education.

During the past academic year I have been a part-time administrative assistant at the Michigan medical school, delving into elderly health care issues under Dr. Millian's supervision. He will be publishing his findings in the American Medical Association's newsletter next November. I am proud to have been a key member of his team.

I feel I have exactly what it takes to do the kind of field research you are conducting. If in fact you are expanding or even thinking of the possibility, I would love to have a conversation and see if or where I might fit in. I will be in your area next week and would like to see if we could meet briefly on Wednesday or Thursday. I'll phone you in a few days to see if you're available.

Yours truly,

Veronica Szerbowski

Comments: Joan has no recent work history that would connect her to her contact in a meaningful way, but her recent assignment at the community college shows she's developed skills she could market to an employer. Her last paragraph even includes a professional endorsement.

Joan Peerzy
1756 Colorado Drive
Pasadena, CA 12345
555 123 4567
peerzy@internetprovider.com

17 March, 2004
Mrs. Solon Hendricks CEO
Acusel, Inc
443 Rosefair Dr.
Pasadena, CA 12345

Dear Mrs. Hendricks,

Congratulations on your recent award as one of the most innovative new companies in Southern California. Those of us following your growth are delighted to hear of your recognition and what was behind it. Miles Fortune, with whom I serve on the Pasadena Employment Training Team, has told me a lot about your business, and how you have grown from three people to over two dozen.

In lieu of a CV I am sending this letter since I don't believe a conventional CV would give a clear picture of what I believe I can offer your firm.

At Pasadena Community College I was a feature writer and interviewed dozens of people for articles. I am an excellent interviewer and 'talent scout' and will be able to help you staff top talent for your future growth. I know how to ask tough questions without giving offence, and to write up accurately what I find out. On the PETT project I helped interview volunteers and assign them to the appropriate work. In this same programme I became very familiar with all the local colleges and training programmes and have good relations with the placement offices.

A good interviewer needs to understand a variety of non-discrimination practices and protocols, and I have just finished researching these requirements on the State website. I am in touch with a member of the local Personnel Resources Association branch and he has checked my knowledge and found it to be thoroughly up to date. He has also helped me familiarize myself with some assessment resources. In finding out about Acusel, I have assumed you do not yet have a full-time Personnel Manager or Recruiter. If this is true, I would like to apply for the position. I can be flexible about my hours in the first months, but will want to work a minimum of 25 hours per week and expand as your needs grow, as I am sure they will.

When would be a good time for us to meet and discuss how I can contribute to your continued success? My schedule next week is flexible. I'll phone you soon.

Sincerely,

Joan Peerzy

CYNTHIA SPENCER
5362 Holliston Road
Fredericksburg, TX 12345
555-123-4567
CS@internetprovider.com

25 May, 2004
Ms. Fredericka Tessani
Texas Publishing
234 Leadwood Boulevard
San Antonio, TX 12345

Dear Ms. Tessani,

I saw your ad in the *San Antonio Star Ledger* (22 May, 2004) and I'm responding. My CV demonstrates a history of editing, and my work has included thousands of hours of proofreading as well.

Why did your ad appeal to me? I love to read the *Star Ledger*. It covers so much of what's important to our city. What most frustrates me in the *Star Ledger*? It's all the mistakes (grammar, syntax, etc.) that slip through. I hate to hear readers make rude remarks about the text in my favourite local paper. It's time I took responsibility.

I would love nothing better than to help build the quality of the *Star Ledger*. I believe the very credibility of any paper is built on its professional integrity, and the closest approximation to perfect grammar, punctuation, spelling, and syntax. Frankly, I follow the *New York Times* daily on the web, but I *buy* the *Star Ledger* daily.

I'd like to spend a few brief minutes with you and show you my work. I'll give you a phone call sometime within the next five days. You will probably have a pretty good response from your ad. There are many writers in this community, but proofreading is in a class by itself.

Sincerely,

Cynthia Spencer

Comments: Cynthia organized her skills and achievements under functional headings in a chronological format. Everything is ordered to match what this job would call for. Her second page gives all the admirable extras that bind her to the community.

CYNTHIA SPENCER

5362 Holliston Road
Fredericksburg, TX 12345
555-123-4567
CS@internetprovider.com

Objective: Proofreading for Newspaper Publisher, Advertising or Other Copy

Skills Summary: Copy editor for over fifteen years:

- 11 published books, two of which are bestsellers in the employee performance field;
- 30-plus workbooks and manuals, training managers and executives in performance coaching;
- A dozen 50-page post-workshop manuals reflecting notes, plans, and strategies from three-day corporate meetings.

1988–present

Editing/Proofreading:

- Co-authored, edited, and proofread new website-downloadable data for 104-page book at: performanceplus.com (2004)
- Noted, assembled details from others' worksheets; rewrote and edited a dozen 35–55-page booklets distributed to participants in workshops done for Harley Telecommunications (2002–2003)
- Edited three major book proposals for established author Dr. Terence Balfour, 50–65 pages each (2003–2004)
- Co-authored complete revision of *Performance Plus* (2000)
- Co-authored and edited *Performance First* (1999)
- Edited revision of bestselling book, *Performance Plus* (1996)

English Instruction:

- As Adjunct Professor, taught college writing to hundreds of first-year students at Monroe College in San Antonio, TX (1999–2002)
- Corrected term papers, masters' theses for hundreds of students in the Monroe College Writing Center (1999–2002)
- Collected dozens of grammar and punctuation books and developed an innovative method to teach grammar and punctuation at the college level.
- Established a reputation as 'The Grammar Queen' at the college, with the quote: '*You won't get anything past her*'.

CYNTHIA SPENCER   555-123-4567   CS@internetprovider.com

Ongoing Development:

- Completed a ten-week online short fiction course on the Internet (WritersPro) with editor's recommendations to proceed to getting published (2004)

Other Items of Interest:

- President, Board of Directors, Share the Wealth, Fredericksburg, TX Not-for-Profit Social Service agency (2001–present)
- President, Board of Directors, Actor's Play Group, Fredericksburg, TX (2002–2004)

Published Books Edited:

- 11 books published from 1988 through 2002: authors – Dr. Stephanie Cartwright and Dr. Terence Balfour.
- Publishers: American Management Association (list available upon request)

Published Books Co-authored:

- *Performance Plus* by Dr. Terence Balfour and Cynthia Spencer, 2000
- *Performance First* by Dr. Terence Balfour and Cynthia Spencer, 1999
- Both books published by American Management Association

Current Co-authoring/ Editing/ Proofreading:

- Complete revision of *Performance Plus* for 2005 publication date.

Education:

MFA   Columbia University, New York, NY
BA   University of Texas at Austin

Comments: Kris's work has all been freelance. The functional format easily shows off his many assignments. As an artist, he uses a more artsy-type font than is usual on CVs.

KRIS PETERSEN   111 Fifth Avenue   (555) 123-4567 home; (555) 123-7456
                    New York, New York 12345   petersen@internetprovider.net

OBJECTIVE: ART DIRECTOR

COMPUTER SKILLS: Adobe Illustrator and PhotoShop, Quark Xpress, Flash, Director

SUMMARY

- Produce product from design concept to completion; known for meeting deadlines.
- Work with customers to develop design intent and specifications.
- Create original design, artwork, and photography for product packaging, trade shows, special events, and training purposes.
- Prepare presentations for top management to feature new product launch.
- Ability to prepare materials for Internet and online marketing.
- Bring projects to completion within budget by managing costs and material selection.

RELATED SKILLS

GRAPHIC DESIGN:
- Develop concepts and execute layout designs including artwork and copy for brochures, catalogues, book lists, print and Internet advertisements.
- Produce designs for textiles, wrapping paper, wallpaper, and silk-screen posters.
- Planned and executed large displays for major metropolitan library to publicize monthly programme and featured displays.
- Interface between customer and printer in a commercial printing shop, assisting in selecting suitable materials, colour, and layout design to meet objectives within budget.

PHOTOGRAPHER/ FREELANCE ARTIST:
- Conferred with client re: budget, objectives, presentation approach, and styles.
- Supervised a commercial photographic studio producing industrial product jobs.
- Created technical illustrations for research publication in the Photo-optics Department of large university using the 'LeRoy' lettering technique.
- Created photography, graphics, and layout for annual reports of BTG, Inc. since 2001.
- Undertook diverse freelance jobs including
  - 3 × 5 foot map of the state university campus   - portrait and product photography
  - large lettering and signage   - slide shows for large institutions

EXPERIENCE:

2000–present	Freelance Artist and Photographer in New York City
1997–2000	STATE UNIVERSITY OF NEW YORK AT BUFFALO, Technical Illustrator
1995–1997	BUFFALO PUBLIC Library, Public Relations Designer
1993–1995	NEWSDAY, INC, Chicago, IL, Layout Artist

EDUCATION:

THE SCHOOL OF VISUAL ARTS, New York, NY, Commercial/Fine Arts
UNIVERSITY OF CHICAGO, Chicago, IL, BA Liberal Arts

Comments: Magdalena has the right history for the chronological format. She has intentionally left out bold type and bullets to make it easier to reformat the CV for the Internet.

MAGDALENA SWIFT
South Webster Street
New Orleans, LA 12345
(555) 123-4567
swift@internetprovider.net

OBJECTIVE: Administrative Assistant in Medium-sized Corporate Environment

SUMMARY: Train office personnel in software upgrades.
Serve as on-site helpdesk to troubleshoot application problems.
Conduct Internet research on technical topics.
Prepare PowerPoint slide shows for conference presentations.
Handle confidential material with discretion.

COMPUTER SKILLS: MS Office Suite, Word, Excel, Access, PowerPoint, Publisher, QuickBooks, Quicken, Peachtree.

PROFESSIONAL EXPERIENCE:

2000–present ADMINISTRATIVE ASSISTANT
Garfield Packaging Company, New Orleans, LA
- Manage three databases generating weekly and monthly reports tracking product lines for executive staff meetings.
- Maintain schedules for five executives arranging meetings and conference calls; screen and route phone calls.
- Train 25 office staff from three departments in latest software upgrades.

1996–2000 TECHNICAL SECRETARY
Schenfield Engineering Corporation, New Orleans, LA
- Maintained technical library alerting staff to articles of interest.
- Researched topics on Internet, edited draft documents for grammar and consistency.
- Served as primary contact person for conference attended by 1,500 scientists; gathered and prepared material for information packs.
- Organized and maintained more than 350 technical files with accounting cross-references.

1994–1996 FINANCIAL AID ASSISTANT, Office of Financial Aid
Professional School for Business, New Orleans, LA
- Documented all incoming records in financial aid database.
- Queried system to create reports on students' status.

1993–1994 OFFICE MANAGER
Salvation Army, New Orleans, LA
- Supervised paid staff of three, and five volunteers.
- Organized fund-raising activities that netted $300,000 for new community centre.
- Recorded donations and pledges from corporations and individuals.

CERTIFICATION: Certified Administrative Professional since 1999
International Association of Administrative Professionals

EDUCATION: PROFESSIONAL SCHOOL FOR BUSINESS, New Orleans, LA

Comments: Suhayla wrote this CV for a specific well-researched job opportunity. Only the targeted format could work here since her chronological history reflects little of the skills she wants to use now.

SUHAYLA MALEK
PO Box 321
Cleveland, OH 12345
(555) 123-4567
malek@internetprovider.com

JOB TARGET:

WORKSHOP FACILITATOR FOR SMALL BUSINESSES THROUGH OHBDC

CAPABILITIES

- Coach groups of retailers in cost-effective solutions to increase productivity.
- Conduct dynamic, in-depth workshops on better business accounting procedures and oversight.
- Develop e-commerce thinking and early strategies for moving into new levels of marketing and sales.
- Solicit and organize multiple funding sources to support and enhance workshop quality.
- Knowledge of Creative Solution Tax Preparation Software, and QuickBooks, Peach tree, and Net Ledger Accounting Software.

ACHIEVEMENTS

- Planned, implemented, and managed a dealership service clinic for 45 current and prospective customers.
- Managed a business office staff of four bookkeepers and computer operators.
- Sold eyeglass frames and other eye care peripherals on the retail level and averaged in the top 10 per cent among the sales staff.
- Assisted in the planning and implementation of several Open House Weekends for 150–250 prospective college students.
- Maintained the accounting records and prepared monthly financial statements for a company with five separate profit centres and average annual gross sales of $19 million.
- Implemented and maintained Net Ledger Application Suite, managing e-commerce accounting, tracking online car accessory sales and inventory for Redmond Car Accessories.
- Prepared a marketing cost-effectiveness study for a college admissions office.

WORK HISTORY:

1995–Present
BOOKKEEPER/CONTROLLER: R.K. Mullen Assoc.   Cleveland, OH
                        Clients:
                        Redmond Car Accessories   Cleveland, OH
                        Madison Ford   Madison, OH
                        Prestige Toyota   Boca Raton, FL

1994–present:
SALES ASSISTANT: Cassidy Optometry   Cleveland, OH
                                                  Boca Raton, FL

EDUCATION:

BS Accounting/Finance   John Carroll University   University Heights, OH

Comments: Johanna emphasizes her functional skills, even in her chrono-logical format, to demonstrate her entrepreneurial capability. This opens her to co-ownership possibilities.

JOHANNA TRACY
11 Sandy Beech Lane
Sarasota, FL 12345
(555) 123-4567 home
(555) 132–4567 business
tracy@internetprovider.net

OBJECTIVE
Design and Develop Successful Spa Concepts

SUMMARY
- Sought after as a speaker in the beauty care field.
- Chosen by a major corporation to assist in the development of a hair and skin care line.
- Authored numerous articles on spa management.
- Track record in promotion and advertising.
- Knowledgeable in ancient Eastern and Western spa concepts.

PROFESSIONAL EXPERIENCE
1992–present   SPA MANAGER, Parfaits Luxor Spa, Sarasota, FL

SPA MANAGEMENT HIGHLIGHTS
- Designed and oversaw construction of a full-service beauty spa.
- Escalated a four-room spa to national recognition; tripled business within seven years.
- Salon selected from several hundred to develop a national hair and skin care line.
- Managed and provided direction to staff of massage therapists, make-up consultants, and beauticians.
- Promoted a contemporary concept of personalized skin care in consultation with advertising agency; sales increased by 40 per cent in one year.
- Research and offer latest modalities including Reiki, aromatherapy, reflexology, manual lymphatic drainage, and other detoxifying body therapies.

TRAINING AND DEVELOPMENT HIGHLIGHTS
- Prepared two salons for national opening; designed floor plan, hired and trained staff, developed service offerings and competitive pricing policy.
- Authored a full training manual encompassing all aspects of spa management and wrote a reference sequel for employers.
- Hosted several on-location TV interviews; quoted in national magazines for several photo shoots; both initial inquiries and repeat bookings increased.
- Conducted successful seminar series for plastic surgeons and dermatologists. Keynote speaker for audience of 1,500; presented to groups of 50.
- Researched knowledge base of beauty experts and hosted monthly meetings to continually upgrade staff.

EDUCATION AND LICENCES
National Academy of Hairdressing: Licensed Cosmetologist and Esthetician
Certification in Training Techniques for Full Service Salons; attended International Symposium, Monte Carlo

Comments: Aaron is switching from public architecture to work in the private sector. This format helps him focus his capability and shape his message to the future.

AARON I. WILSON   531 Olive Street   (555) 123-4567
    Des Moines, IA 12345   wilson@internetprovider.com

JOB TARGET: Licensed Architect in a Private Firm Specializing in Commercial Design

CAPABILITIES:

- Oversee project from feasibility research to final construction.
- Prepare cost analysis and land use studies.
- Interpret commercial building codes, zoning laws, and fire regulations.
- Design super-sized fast food facilities, adhering to local design modes.
- Communicate with planning boards, negotiating local and client needs.
- Adhere strictly to all construction safety standards.
- Propose alterations and renovations of many styles of architecture.
- Consider sound and lighting needs of specialized buildings such as concert facilities and libraries.

ACCOMPLISHMENTS:

- Determined space requirements and designed renovation of former secondary school building to county offices; project completed on time and within budget.
- Researched energy efficiency of county buildings and designed alteration recommendations; reduced annual energy expenditures by 10 per cent.
- Designed

office buildings	health care facilities
industrial complexes	power plants
health centres	schools
courts	libraries
police stations	access roads

- Planned, organized, directed, and reviewed all architectural and engineering functions in a large, densely populated county.
- Participated in pre-design meetings with developers to resolve issues with feasibility and environmental impact study requirements.
- Conducted a study to determine methods to reduce exposure of public building to terrorism attack with minimal effect on the services to county residents.

PROFESSIONAL EXPERIENCE:

1997–present   COUNTY ARCHITECT, Cumberland, IA
    Cumberland County Department of Buildings and Grounds

1990–1997   ASSOCIATE ARCHITECT
    Carl. N. Tyne Associates, Des Moines, IA

EDUCATION/CERTIFICATION:

1992   Certified Architect, National Council of Architectural Registration Board (NCARB). Licensed in IA and MO.
1989   Bachelor of Arts in Architecture, Grinnell College, Grinnell, IA

Comments: Michael's work history suits the chronological format. Note how he emphasizes his job titles *over* employer names. He also eliminates a summary statement since his current job has all the right keywords.

MICHAEL JAMES FORDER
4468 Elmwood Street #232
Minneapolis, MN 12345
555-123-4567
forder@internetprovider.net

OBJECTIVE: DIRECTOR OF OPERATIONS IN HEALTH CARE

EXPERIENCE:

2000–present   OPERATIONS SUPERVISOR
Raleigh-Rhinestone Health Care Centers, Minneapolis, MN

- Supervised the purchase and distribution of supplies and equipment for three sites with annual budget of $4 million.
- Developed database to track current inventory and fill back orders; system increased utilization of inventory on hand and flagged items for quantity purchase; reduced costs by 20 per cent.
- Negotiated purchase agreements with vendors to establish best pricing and to return obsolete inventory for full credit.
- Implemented procedures for collecting and transporting hazardous waste in compliance with state standards.

1997–2000   SUPPLY, PROCUREMENT, AND DISTRIBUTION TECHNICIAN
St. Alphonsus Hospital, Minneapolis, MN

- Established and maintained stock levels of medical and surgical supplies for a 300-bed hospital including casualty department, surgery, and outpatient clinic.
- Purchased all stock for the central supply department, maintaining adequate levels for emergencies.
- Checked, cleaned, and sterilized instruments used for surgery and the casualty department in compliance with state codes.

1992–1997   RADIO ANNOUNCER, KSZT
St. Paul, MN
- Wrote and produced commercial copy for local sponsors.
- Prepared and broadcast an eight-hour radio music programme; compiled copy for hourly news and sports.
- Increased listeners by 20 per cent with games and sponsor-donated prizes.

EDUCATION:

AA, Business Administration
MANKATO TECHNICAL COLLEGE, Mankato, MN

Comments: Ed uses the targeted format since he's looking for project consulting. He also wants to de-emphasize the 'closed' employment dates, as he was laid off.

Edward P. Lockhardt
222 Sandy Court
Tucson, AZ 12345
(555) 123-4567
lockhardt@internetprovider.com

OBJECTIVE: Manage Communication Projects for Conferences

CAPABILITIES:

- Meet conference planners to assess communication requirements.
- Assure that equipment meets technical specifications of space/locations.
- Negotiate prices to keep projects in line with budget requirements.
- Coordinate activities with equipment suppliers and crews to minimize staff down time and contain costs.
- Interview and hire crews with required skill-sets.
- Supervise work crews for set up/breakdown.
- Orient technical operators to task and programme.

ACHIEVEMENTS:

- Assessed phone system networks for new installations or expansion capability of existing installations.
- Reviewed specifications required for voice and data telecommunication lines.
- Prepared cost estimates for both equipment and labour.
- Negotiated preliminary contracts for equipment, installation, and service.
- Evaluated problems to determine probable causes and send repair staff to return customers to full service in minimum time.
- Monitored staff at multiple locations to ensure that all projects were on schedule and within budget.
- Interfaced with customers to assure that communication requirements were met and staff had provided excellent customer service.
- Met with upper management to inform them of current project time lines and proposed projects under consideration.
- Relayed needs that customers have identified for future service expansion.

PROFESSIONAL EXPERIENCE:

1993–2004   Technical Supervisor, Tucson Region Communications, Tucson, AZ

EDUCATION: Southern Arizona Community College, Communications Certificate

Comments: Jessica has an ideal work history for the chronological format. Note how she uses bold and italic type, and caps, as well as white space to enhance readability of otherwise dense information.

JESSICA L. SMITHERS

1 Terriance Court • Wappingers Falls, NY 12345 • (555) 123-4567 • smithers@internetprovider.com

OBJECTIVE:

Project Manager / Team Leader or Computer Programmer
Systems Analyst to Leverage Skills at Creating Solid Applications

SUMMARY:

Senior-level programmer/analyst with extensive experience in C++ and object-oriented programming. Skilled in all phases of project development including team leader, design, coding, testing, debugging, documentation, installation, support, and maintenance.

Currently pursuing a Master's Degree in Computer Science – Software Development.

SKILLS:

- Microsoft Visual C++ using MFC, IBM VisualAge C++ using the IBM Open Class Libraries, C, Pascal.

- MS Windows (95, 98, NT), OS/2 (1.2 to Warp 4), MS-DOS, UNIX.

- SQL, EHLLAPI, OS/2 LAN Server/Re quester, PVCS, OS/2 Presentation Manager, IPF, Vyper Help, MS Project, MS Excel.

PROFESSIONAL HISTORY:

SENIOR PROGRAMMER/ANALYST   Computer Consortium NY, NY (1998 to present)
Consultant to Dell Computers, White Plains, NY

Assignment No. 2:   Electron Beam Lithography Tool Software

Develop the software to run a new, state-of-the-art, Electron Beam Lithography tool as part of a large team of engineers and programmers. Individual assignment included developing software in Microsoft Visual C++ using MFC, running under Windows NT.

Highlights:

- Completed a requirements document, time estimate, and detailed specification for rewriting a set of programs that takes tool parameters from an engineer and prepares them for use in configuring the tool.

- Migrated the old back-end C software to a Visual C++ console application.

- Rewrote code to use classes for the major parts of the program to move it in an object-oriented direction and to produce configuration files in a new format. Tested and verified these by hand.

- Coded, tested, and debugged the user interface of a program to display status messages. This is a dialog application using a tabbed control for list controls.

Assignment No. 1:   Step and Repeat Substrate Tester Software

As part of a three-person team, developed a GUI to control processing for a step and repeat substrate tester. The project was designed using IBM's Visual Modeling Technique – a hybrid of several object-oriented design methodologies.

- Included such features as a drag-and-drop interface to initiate testing and tool configuration.
- Code interfaced with a database program and a low-level tool-control program on the back end using custom-designed interfaces.
- Program is multi-threaded and was coded in an object-oriented manner in IBM Visual Age C++ running under OS/2 Warp 4. The program is currently in production.

Highlights:

- Designed, coded, tested, debugged, and documented a set of GUI notebooks and dialogs used to input tool and product configuration data for the test-control program.
- Created help text for the GUI portion of the application using the Vyper Help utility (an IPF editor). Using this as starting point, created a User's Guide.
- Created technical documentation for the project.

SENIOR SYSTEMS PROGRAMMER   Marlboro Telecomm, Bethpage, NY (1995–1998)

- Clarified requirements, created and documented design for all projects.
- Held design reviews, created project assessment documents.
- Coordinated coding, wrote documentation, and released new versions for production. Produced production and system documentation.
- Designed, coded, tested, and debugged new programs and modified existing programs using primarily C, EHLLAPI, and SQL.
- Troubleshot and fixed PC, LAN and order-entry production problems.

Highlights:

- Worked as a project leader coordinating the work of two other programmers in developing new functionality for the front end of the business order entry system. This was an OS/2 PM notebook written in C++ running in a client-server environment.
- Installed and configured server and PC software needed to run the program.
- Produced weekly project status report for management.

EDUCATION:

Master's Degree in progress – Simpson College, Beacon, NY
Subject: Computer Science – Software Development
BA Albany College of SUNY, Albany NY

AS Wharton University, Penbrooke, CT
Subject: Computer and Information Science

Comments: Randall is moving up to management, so he can best highlight his skills and accomplishments from three jobs through the functional CV.

RANDALL RISSMAN
447 Christy Street
Little Rock, AK 12345
(555) 123-4567; FAX (555) 123- 6745
rissman@internetprovider.net

OBJECTIVE: BUILDING MANAGER Combining Skills in Mechanical Engineering and Stationary Engineering

SUMMARY:

- Troubleshoot and repair heating, ventilating, and air conditioning systems.
- Operate, maintain, repair, and refurbish boilers, turbines, generators, and diesel engines.
- Understand current building codes, safety standards, and environmental regulations.
- Prepare budgets and cost estimates for maintenance needs and new equipment.

GENERAL ADMINISTRATION:

- Coordinate plant service activities, including installation, maintenance, and repair of mechanical and air handler equipment for a 30,000 square foot data processing centre.
- Develop and monitor preventive maintenance schedules to assure that facilities equipment is in compliance with OSHA as well as environmental and building codes.
- Prepared equipment for insurance inspection; achieved lowest rate scale.
- Supervise work of a turbine operator and air conditioning and refrigeration mechanic.
- Prepare cost and manpower estimates to install equipment for energy-saving projects.

STATIONARY ENGINEERING/ BUILDING MAINTENANCE:

- Monitored computerized controls and meters to ensure that facilities equipment was operating in a safe and efficient manner and to control energy consumption.
- Repaired and maintained all mechanical aspects of diesel engines, turbines, and generators including bearing and valve replacement, pump overhauls, and general machine repairs.
- Made extensive steam line alternations and additions for a conversion to natural gas.
- Installed industrial services, equipment, and wiring under the supervision of a licensed electrical contractor.
- Troubleshot equipment failures in all mechanical systems of HVAC equipment.
- Performed maintenance schedule including cleaning and lubricating of parts, testing of air quality, and equipment efficiency.

PROFESSIONAL EXPERIENCE:

1997–present   MAINTENANCE TECHNICIAN, Technicians, Inc., Little Rock, AK
1994–1997   OILER/MAINTENANCE MACHINIST, Northern Railroad, Reading, NJ
1992–1994   ELECTRICIAN'S ASSISTANT, Lewis Electric Company, Reading, NJ

EDUCATION:

1996 Blue-Seal License – Stationary Engineering, Charleston Technical School, Middlesex, NJ
1995 BS Mechanical Engineering, Trenton State College, Trenton, NJ

Comments: Even though he has a progressive work history, Marcus is changing his journalistic focus to the music industry. Since he has only freelance experience, he chose the functional CV.

MARCUS T. YARDLEY
340 Harding Place, Apt. 47
Chicago, IL 12345
(555) 123-4567
yardley@internetprovider.net

OBJECTIVE: Reporter with a National Music Industry Publication, Producing Quality Stories Combining Journalism Ability and Knowledge of the Music Industry.

SUMMARY:

- Reporter experienced in covering national, local, and regional topics.
- Contribute to news coverage decisions as assistant editor.
- Effectively work a news beat while meeting tight production deadlines.
- Monitor trends and issues in the music industry; work with developed sources.
- Adept at Internet research.

RELATED EXPERIENCE:

NEWSPAPER JOURNALISM

- Provided regional political reporting for a metropolitan newspaper; circulation 130,000.
- Covered the City of Suffolk, VA, including zoning and planning boards and city council.
- Wrote articles on regional issues: housing, transport, and economic development.
- Developed media strategy and campaigns to attract coverage of housing issues such as the Low-Income Housing Credit and other non-profit development efforts.
- Reported on court proceedings in five suburban Chicago-area Circuit Court districts and US District Court. Tracked topics and maintained issues record.
- Produced spot coverage of police, politics, and public relations.
- Participated in editorial decision making and supervised general assignment reporters.
- Researched stories on Illinois state politics including state legislature and local political races.

MUSIC INDUSTRY JOURNALISM

- Developed in-depth understanding of the pop music industry to report on record industry news.
- Wrote feature articles about the relationship of pop music industry politics and political culture.
- Covered live concerts and CD releases, interviewing musicians for weekly features.
- Published articles in suburban *Chicago Tribune*, and music industry magazines *Catharsis* and *Jet Lag*.
- Founded, edited, and published a music magazine, *Better Than Anything*, in Urbana, IL; circulation 25,000 in 2003.

PROFESSIONAL HISTORY:

1997–present   ASSISTANT EDITOR/STAFF WRITER, *Windy City Views*, Chicago, IL

1995–1997   REPORTER, *Suffolk News Daily Press*, Suffolk, VA

1993–1995   REPORTER, COURTROOM AND GENERAL ASSIGNMENT
                 Chicago City News Bureau, Chicago, IL

EDUCATION:

University of Illinois, Champaign-Urbana, IL   BA Political Science

Comments: James chose the targeted format to highlight capability for future work in a fast-changing industry and to replace the summary statement. This format also de-emphasizes the fact that he is no longer with his last employer.

JAMES D. HALLINAN
442 Wolff Road
Boston, MA 12345
(555) 123-4567
hallinan@internetprovider.com

JOB TARGET: PRINTED CIRCUIT DESIGNER

CAPABILITIES:

- Design printed circuits using PADS; update component library with latest technical information.
- Examine engineering schematics from View Logic CAD.
- Work with engineer on circuit design and submit soft copies to manufacturer for circuit board build.
- Review bill of materials generated from CAD program for accuracy, updating component library as required.
- Design cables using specialized computer-aided design systems.
- Evaluate final product after build using analog and digital test equipment.
- Skilled in use of AutoCAD and specialized design systems.

ACCOMPLISHMENTS:

- Modified circuit board designs to optimize reliability, manufacturability, heat transfer, and noise reduction, and to minimize signal paths.
- Increased ease of servicing circuit boards by critiquing subsequent engineering schematic designs until prototypes and schematics were ready for release to manufacturing.
- Generated unique library attributes for components using PADS system resulting in PC boards being designed in a timely manner.
- Designed frames to house electronic subassemblies.
- Served as liaison between manufacturing and engineering.

EXPERIENCE:

1997–2004	SENIOR DESIGNER/GRAPHICS DESIGN SPECIALIST Options, Inc., Marlborough, MA
1994–1997	SENIOR DESIGNER Harrigan Corporation, Boston, MA
1990–1994	ELECTRO-MECHANICAL DESIGNER, Modular Products Finebeck Computer Control, Boston, MA

EDUCATION:

- Programming Lab View for Circuit Debug, C++, and PADS Layout Design, Nashua Community College, New Hampshire.
- Analog/Digital Circuit Design Certificate, BOTS Learning Center, Boston, MA.
- AAS – Electronic Engineering, Berkshire Community College.

Comments: Elektra's entire working career is with one employer, so she used the chronological format and highlighted her skill areas into functional categories.

ELEKTRA HUNDHAUSEN
25 Wilmington Walkway · Chicago, IL 12345
(555) 123-4567
hundhausen@internetprovider.net

OBJECTIVE: FASHION BUYER FOR A SMALL RETAIL CLOTHING FRANCHISE

SUMMARY:

- Annual buying responsibility over nine years for $10 million in sales volume.
- Ability to make key financial decisions.
- Capability to take calculated risks to increase profitability.
- Develop business strategies to drive sales, maintain sales quotas, and increase profit margin.
- Predict customer demand by researching and analysing economic and industry trends.
- Administrative, supervisory, and training skills.
- Adept in Internet research and e-commerce strategies.
- Fluent in French.

PROFESSIONAL EXPERIENCE

1992–present   MATHEWS SHEFFIELD & COMPANY: Chicago, IL
                 Assistant Fashion Buyer (1994–present)
                 Purchasing: Senior Clerical Assistant (1992–1994)

PURCHASING: RETAIL AND CATALOGUE

- Select merchandise for three medium-sized retail stores and catalogue specializing in women's clothing; identify hottest trends in styles and colours.
- Advance promotional strategies by planning product assortment and analysing current sales and inventory records including merchandise on order.
- Develop and maintain vendor partnership, negotiating discounts for volume purchases and shipping expenses.
- Determine price and merchandising strategy including mark-up and mark-down action.
- Examine merchandise to assure product meets order specifications for size ranges, style, colour, and quality.
- Initiated changes in store product balance to attract new customers and increase sales; new mix of products increased traffic by 22 per cent and sales by 15 per cent.
- Compute cost analysis; compare cost with quarterly sales reports.
- Maintain constant inventory control by analysing data from computerized point-of-sale system.

ELEKTRA HUNDHAUSEN   (555) 123-4567   hundhausen@internetprovider.net

---

PRODUCT DEVELOPMENT

- Analyse merchandise for defects in design and material to assure quality manufacturing standards are met and negotiate improvements as needed.
- Investigate comparative merchandise in competing stores for reports to guide future buying decisions.
- Initiated talks with producer to develop and test-market private-label merchandise to aid in creating brand identity; survey indicated 15 per cent increase in brand recognition.
- Locate new supply sources; evaluate based on price, quality, and selection; negotiate price and delivery schedules.

ADMINISTRATION

- Supervise maintenance of all office records, systems, and purchase orders using QuickBooks and dedicated retail software.
- Act as liaison between vendor sources and retail stores.
- Coordinate retail and catalogue merchandise selections and promotions for customer convenience; introduced and maintained Intranet links between retail stores and catalogue.
- Negotiate and prepare contracts to buy merchandise for three brick-and-mortar stores and Internet catalogue; create file with full back-up data for future analysis.
- Use computerized purchasing system to submit orders electronically.
- Execute product-pricing strategies to increase sales without reducing profit.
- Oversee advertising department timing on delivery of merchandise to ensure that advertised specials are available by sale dates.
- Respond to escalated customer complaints and service enquiries promptly; use customer contact as an opportunity to gain and retain customer loyalty.
- Trained employees from the Buyer's Assistant Training Programme increasing stores' reputation for customer service.
- Reduced staff turnover by hiring and training staff with enthusiasm for retail and implementing incentive and bonus programmes.

EDUCATION:

1996   AA in Fashion Merchandising   Stevens Sturtevant College, Chicago, IL

Comments: Margaret's targeted format supports her consulting objective, allowing her to feature capabilities for future work that would otherwise be hidden in a chronological CV.

MARGARET SILVER   2363 El Camino Real   (555) 123-4567 (days)
                      Palo Alto, CA 12345   (555) 123-4657 (evenings)
                                                 silver@internetprovider.net

JOB TARGET: TELECOMMUNICATIONS CONSULTING MANAGER

CAPABILITIES:

- Communicate technical information to all levels of management and business customers to assist in decision making on advanced communication services.
- Manage details under pressure in complex and competitive environments.
- Identify demand for new products and potential markets.
- Develop market strategies to guide new product promotion and pricing to diverse market segments.
- Research competing products to maintain competitive product lines.
- Knowledgeable in technology of wire line, wireless and third-generation wireless access, telephony, and various message communication services.

ACCOMPLISHMENTS:

- Served as liaison between customers and engineers to tailor voice and data communication systems to customer needs; customer base growth of 20 per cent in 1999.
- Received outstanding sales award for creating $2.5 million in new revenue in 2001; maintained 120 per cent of annual objective in 1999, 2001, and 2002.
- Managed $6.5 million of Pacific Bell annual revenue; maintained accounts of 110 business customers, identifying upgraded products to better meet their needs.
- Trained customer sales representatives in both technical and consultative sales communication skills; department consistently exceeded sales objectives by 18 per cent.

PROFESSIONAL EXPERIENCE:

1996–present   ACCOUNT EXECUTIVE, TELECOMMUNICATIONS   (1998–present)
               CUSTOMER SALES REPRESENTATIVE   (1996–1998)

               Pacific Bell Telephone Company, Burlingame, CA
               (formerly Bell Communication Systems)

1992–1996   STORE MANAGER, Thompson's Gifts, Palo Alto, CA (1994–1996)
               DEPARTMENT MANAGER, Lieberman's, Menlo Park, CA (1992–1996)

EDUCATION:

BS Business/Marketing	University of San Francisco, CA
Management and Technical Courses,	Pacific Bell Training Programme
- brand and product management	- sales management evaluation
- interactive marketing	- organizational communication
- telephony	- laser and fibre optic technology

AFFILIATIONS: Sales and Marketing Executives International, member since 1997.

Comments: Chris's career is perfect for the chronological format: no gaps, progressive career in the same field.

CHRIS ADAMSON DUNCAN
42 Markham Place
London, W31 6PD
(055-5) 123-4567
duncan@internetprovider.net

OBJECTIVE: Finance, Vice President of Multinational Corporation to Apply Expertise in International Banking and Monetary Policy.

SUMMARY:

- Multilingual: French, Italian, and German.
- Develop policies to comply with Securities and Exchange Commission rules.
- Understand protocols of the World Bank and International Monetary Fund.
- Track record in evaluating global economic policy, and analysing fluctuations of foreign economic climate, the euro, and US dollar policy.
- Comfortable with foreign travel and customs.

PROFESSIONAL EXPERIENCE:

1996–present   CHASE INVESTMENT BANK, London, UK

MANAGING DIRECTOR

- Evaluate non-market forces such as political events and relative stability of foreign governments to determine impact on current policy and recommendations.
- Determine strategies and tactics for negotiations with foreign business partners; successfully closed $350 million deal timed to take advantage of favourable monetary and interest rate policy.
- Establish and maintain significant contact with domestic and foreign subsidiaries and institutional investors in emerging markets.
- Supervise accounting and reporting systems for branches in United Kingdom.
- Arranged a $500 million multiple option facility for the Kingdom of Spain.
- Originated ten Eurobond issues throughout the EEC for US and European multinationals.
- Arranged and syndicated a ten-year Swiss Franc $100 million loan swap transaction.

1989–1996   THE CHASE MANHATTAN BANK, N.A., New York, NY

VICE PRESIDENT, SWISS INSTITUTIONAL BANKING (1994–1996)

- Managed an eleven-person team overseeing employer's relationship with 150 Swiss and Lichtenstein banks; provided guidance and oversight to investment managers.
- Ensured compliance with US and Swiss regulatory agencies.
- Negotiated over $100 million in new documentary business.
- Coordinated five-year European Strategic Plan.
- Honoured by Consortium of Swiss Bankers for effective planning.

VICE PRESIDENT, INTERNATIONAL TRADE FINANCE (1992—1994)
- Created and implemented innovative approach to extending credit in conjunction with the World Bank.
- Oversaw investment of funds and managed associated risks to increase profitability of investments.
- Developed new financial risk participation product to increase trade financial business; product marketing brought $25 million in new business in first quarter.
- Monitored investment performance and worked with other units to maximize return on investment; improved performance by 25 per cent in two years.
- Coordinated employer's worldwide financial activities with World Bank and International Monetary Fund.

SECOND VICE PRESIDENT, CORPORATE FOREIGN DIRECT (1989—1992)
- Managed employer's relationship with US subsidiaries of French and Swiss multinationals.
- Developed $30 million portfolio of high-quality financial assets by forecasting future trends to increase profitability of investments.
- Supervised cash management and executed capital-raising strategies to support expansion of portfolio and operations.
- Funded acquisition of Atlantic Bank Group by executing capital-raising strategies to support expansion into new market; realized 25 per cent increase in profits within two years.

EDUCATION:

New York University, New York, NY
Master's, Business Administration

Williams College, Williamstown, MA
BA, International Studies

MEMBER:

International Bankers Consortium, Geneva, Switzerland

Comments: Bradley's summary statement says it all. He could also have chosen a targeted format, but the chronological highlights his excellent career growth.

BRADLEY SHAW
331 Fort Salonga Road
Northport, NY 12345
(555) 123-4567
shaw@internetprovider.net

OBJECTIVE:

CONSULTING – MATERIALS SCIENCE, INSTRUMENT APPLICATIONS

SUMMARY:

- Organize and maintain analytical laboratory facilities for the characterization of metals, alloys, ceramics, polymers, plastics, fluids, and lubricants.
- Manage projects in materials testing including technical staff supervision and budget maintenance and reporting.
- Research Consultant to US government including NASA.
- Conversant with computer modelling programs for technical analysis.
- Hold three patents and two patent disclosures.

PROFESSIONAL EXPERIENCE:

1993–present   SUPERVISOR, ANALYTICAL CHEMISTRY LAB
                Garrison-Weist Corporation, Garden City, NY

PROJECT DEVELOPMENT

- Create computer models to replicate and manipulate material characteristics in non-destructive testing studies to research the effects of corrosive environmental conditions.
- Study the effects of solvents, chemical pollutants, and oil on ocean ecosystems; developed techniques for more efficient clean-up procedures to lessen cost and environmental damage.
- Designed specialized lab including power requirements, compressed air, and other gases and fluids; ensured implementation of OSHA safety standards.
- Conduct corrosion and out-gassing studies on ceramic components for NASA.
- Developed a procedure to remove carbon inclusions from diamonds; process saved 25 per cent over previous technology.

PROJECT MANAGEMENT

- Supervise nine graduate chemists in an analytical chemistry lab; provide even project distribution in accordance with individual skills and deadline priorities.
- Provide technical problem-solving support to graduate research assistants.
- Serve as liaison with customers to determine testing needs and specifications; present periodic presentations on work progress.
- Provide staffing, equipment, and cost estimates to upper management.
- Issue monthly reports on progress of projects and cost analysis; maintain projects within budget constraints.

BRADLEY SHAW   (555) 123-4567   shaw@internetprovider.net

1991–1993   TECHNICAL CONSULTANT
            R.M.T. Surface Chemicals, Northport, NY

- Purchased all technical equipment used in highly specialized test laboratory; negotiated specifications, price, and product support agreements.
- Conducted corrosion and out-gassing studies on semi-conductor packaging including plastics, ceramics, and metals.
    - Analysed leakage of electronic component seals after environmental stress tests, thermal cycling, and temperature and humidity exposure.
    - Studied environmental content surrounding unit under test to determine if out-gassing was within specification range.
- Conducted comparative analysis of surfaces in electroplated and anodized parts to determine permeability.

1990–1991   TECHNICAL CONSULTANT
            Durell Electronics, Bethpage, NY

- Set up procedures and special techniques for the non-destructive testing and analysis of integrated circuits, printed circuit boards, semiconductor devices, laser materials, and internal components.
- Developed an automated process with procedural manual for the non-destructive testing for failure analysis of integrated circuits so that semi-skilled staff could complete product test; saved 30 per cent in staffing needs.

EDUCATION

HOFSTRA UNIVERSITY, New York
MS: Chemistry
MS: Materials Engineering
BS: Oceanography

LONG ISLAND UNIVERSITY, New York
Business Administration (25 credits completed)

Comments: Kelly covers keywords for scanning in her combined objective and summary statement. The objective and the chronological titles are in bold fonts to attract the reader's immediate attention.

KELLY M. JONES
22 Tiparillo Circle
Montgomery, AL 12345
(555) 123-4567
jones@internetprovider.com

OBJECTIVE AND SUMMARY

Corporate Foundation Manager – Coordinate Philanthropic Programmes to Meet Established Goals and Assure Regulatory Compliance.

- Experienced non-profit financial manager with expertise in understanding of and compliance with government regulations.
- Skilled in developing guidelines and procedures to meet organization goals.
- Successfully managed benefits programmes to control costs with minimal reduction in services valued by employees.
- Produced full range of public relations materials from newsletters and newspaper articles to annual reports.

PROFESSIONAL EXPERIENCE

1995–present **Director of Finance and Operations**
Montgomery County Career Center, Montgomery, AL

- Manage fiscal reporting for $10 million federal grant.
- Develop financial policy and procedures to assure compliance with government regulations and reporting requirements; submitted timely reports.
- Manage the Management Information System department, training all employees in new database system developed to track outcomes.
- Coordinate the organization and state databases to produce reports required by several levels of government.
- Conduct an organization-wide survey to determine staff benefit needs
- Negotiate with providers to create a custom benefits package at no additional cost to employee or employer.

1989–1995 **Controller/Chief Financial Officer**
Alabama Employer's Federal Credit Union, Montgomery, AL

- Coordinated and directed investments to ensure financial goals were met.
- Directed preparation of reports on financial condition to regulatory agency.
- Reorganized accounting department, saving $85K annually.
- Oversaw the selection and training of all department staff.

EDUCATION   Southern Christian University, Montgomery, AL – BA in Accounting

Comments: Marty's career history is ideal for the chronological format. He
leaves out a summary since his first two paragraphs cover the same facts.

Marty Harrowood
2456 Sagebrush Lane ◆ Salt Lake City, UT 12345
Home: (555) 123-4567 ◆ Office: (555) 213-4675, ext.56
harrwood@internetprovider.com

OBJECTIVE: Purchasing Consultant to a Medium-sized Company

WORK EXPERIENCE:

1993–present SULLIVAN MINING & ALLOYS CO. Salt Lake City, UT
1997–present **Manager, Chemicals Purchasing**
- Manage a corporate procurement group that purchases the major chemical raw materials for over 100 consuming plants in the US.
- Commodity responsibility includes pulp and paper chemicals, plastic resins, inks, waxes, coatings, solvents, plastic film and sheet, and lignosulfonates.
- Direct six professional buyers and non-exempt programmes with annual savings over $1 million.
- Initiated programme in support of Hazardous Waste Disposal project. Participated in strategy planning and negotiations for key raw materials.

1993–1997 **Materials Manager**

- Designed and implemented necessary systems and procedures to establish purchasing activities between corporate purchasing and SM&A.

1988–1993 NEMO CHEMICALS & PHARMACEUTICALS, Denver, CO
  Purchasing Agent

- Negotiated for $40 billion of specialty and commodity raw materials.
- Contributed significantly (by 22 per cent) to NC&P's cost reduction programme.
- Performed liaison function between corporate purchasing and Consolidated of Canada, Ltd.
- Implemented programme to improve reporting systems between plants and purchasing.

EDUCATION:

Various management courses sponsored by Sullivan Mining & Alloys Co., and Nemo Chemicals & Pharmaceuticals, Ltd.

Westminster College, Salt Lake City, UT

Comments: Janann's chronological CV highlights a steady career history with no gaps and continuous growth. Her current job leads perfectly into her career objective.

Janann Bethany Howard
7877 Morrissey Avenue
Pleasantville, NY 12345
(555) 123-4567
howard@.internetprovider.com

OBJECTIVE: Software Sales Management

2002–present STOCKWOOD COMMUNICATIONS, Yonkers, NY
Programme Manager
- Manage a customer service/marketing programme targeting the company's top customers nationally, resulting in $775K sales/year.
- Identify opportunities, formulate strategies, and implement plans to stimulate sales of company's microcomputer software product line.
- Supervise staff of six; develop and promote internal talent.

1995–2002 CORLEY HEALTH ASSOCIATES, Bend, OR
Senior Administrator
- Developed decision papers for trustees and executives of $360 million budget HMO.
- Identified organizational impact of issues and recommended alternative options.
- Edited managerial materials for presentation to board, consulting with senior-level executives in developing information.

Assistant Office Director
- Supervised staff of twelve.
- Oversaw transition of office to fully automated office system, resulting in increased staff productivity and higher morale. Wrote newsletters and speeches for trustees.
- Developed and refined a computerized database management program, improving the speed in retrieving information used in decision making.
- Managed a reduction in staff due to organizational budget cuts, maintaining productivity standard with fewer staff members.

1990–1995 AMERICAN ASSOCIATION OF RETIRED PERSONS, Washington, DC
Legislative Specialist
- Researched, analysed, and reported legislative interests of association's membership.
- Organized association's first formal legislative correspondence section, improving response time to over 1,500 letters received each month.

EDUCATION

1995 UNIVERSITY OF WASHINGTON, Seattle, WA
Master of Public Administration

ELMIRA COLLEGE, Elmira, NY
BA in Political Science, cum laude

Comments: Nicole's expertise is well expressed in her summary, and her choice to break down the specifics into categories is well served by the functional format.

NICOLE S. GARRIST
331 Cliffside Estates Way
Portland, OR 12345
(555) 123-4567
garrist@internetprovider.net

OBJECTIVE: Claims Director in the Insurance Industry to Reduce Corporate Claims Costs

SUMMARY:
- Negligence and no-fault litigation experience in car insurance industry.
- Analyse contracts recommending changes in policy wording to conform to legal precedents of current court decisions; knowledge of DOT regulations.
- Review and revise insurance policy wording to reduce unwarranted claims.
- Advise management on legal rights and precedents in upcoming cases, submitting cost analysis of litigation versus payment.
- Trial experience: represented corporation and clients at depositions and in court.
- Adept at focusing database searches, thoroughly studying topic while controlling search costs; comfortable with automated litigation technology including Doculex.

RELEVANT EXPERIENCE

INSURANCE LAW:
- Protect company from unwarranted claims by studying pattern of claims filed and revising contracts as needed to close loopholes.
- Research the legality of claims filed to prevent undue payments; evaluate and negotiate claims effecting cost-effective settlements.
- Evaluate risk exposure associated with vehicles and equipment; make recommendations to determine underwriting policy and rates.
- Study and interpret complex coverage issues, claims, and federal and state legislation to determine effect on current and future contracts.

CORPORATE LAW:
- Prepare legal opinions and memoranda involving coverage interpretation to reduce corporate liability and exposure to legal suits.
- Draft case summaries and reports; analyse contracts and release papers.
- Acted as agent for corporations in insurance and property transactions.

PROPERTY LAW:
- Planned and executed property transactions with attention to taxation issues.
- Instituted title searches; drew up deeds, mortgages, and leases.
- Acted as trustee of property and held funds for investment.

PROFESSIONAL EXPERIENCE:

1995–present	INSURANCE SERVICES LEGAL OFFICE SUPERVISOR
	Commercial Underwriters Company, Inc., Portland, OR
1992–1995	ATTORNEY, Warren and Buckley, PC, Portland, OR

EDUCATION: LLB – Insurance Law, University of Oregon Law School
BA – History, University of Oregon

Comments: Lawrence's work history allows him a chronological CV, but he chose the functional format to highlight the variety of his accomplishments in two different areas of expertise.

LAWRENCE F. O'TOOLE   3 Greenwald Avenue   (555) 123-4567
                          Tumwater, WA 12345   otoole@internetprovider.net

OBJECTIVE: SENIOR GEOTECHNICAL PROJECT MANAGER

SUMMARY:

- Experience using computer modelling and digital mapping of water and oil flow.
- Knowledge of federal, state, and EPA regulations; ability to work with regulatory staff.
- Testified numerous times before the State Oil and Gas Commissions of Texas and Louisiana as an expert witness.
- Ability to clarify complex technical material in written and oral communications.
- Business skills: set strategic goals and deliver projects within budget guidelines.

RELEVANT EXPERIENCE:

GEOLOGY

- Participate in site characterization studies for industrial and oil refinery installations.
- Use seismic soundings to locate oil pockets in sub-surface rock layers and complex bedrock environments; computer model mapping used for drilling decisions.
- Direct drilling, logging, and coring activities during well-site operations; keep boring logs to accurately identify sediment layers.
- Evaluate, examine, and prepare drill cuttings and core samples.
- Conduct surface mapping investigations and take field measurements to study rock and sediment samples.

HAZARDOUS WASTE

- Certified in OSHA Safety and Health Training for hazardous waste site investigations.
- Understanding of CERCLA, RCRA, and EPA regulations.
- Proficient in the theory and application of gamma, geophysical, and resistivity logs.
- Produce alternative strategies for remediation of hazardous waste sites to comply with all federal, state, and local regulations.

PROFESSIONAL EXPERIENCE:

1998–present   GEOTECHNICAL CONSULTANT, Exxon, USA, Inc., Tumwater, WA
1995–1998   GEOLOGICAL CONSULTANT, MHQ Corporation, Tumwater, WA
1992–1995   AREA GEOLOGIST, Kufacker Exploration Co., Walla Walla, WA

EDUCATION:

Hazardous Materials Management Certified   Tumwater Technical Center, Tumwater, WA
MS – Geophysics; BS – Geology;   Missouri School of Mines, Rolla, MO

Comments: Juliet's chronological CV shows to advantage with functional categories highlighted. Note that at the bottom under 'Publications', her published materials are italicized.

CHRONOLOGICAL CV

Juliet Thatcher
269 West End Avenue, Apt 57
New York, New York 12345
(555) 123-4567
thatcher@internetprovider.net

OBJECTIVE: HOUSE COUNSEL in Medium to Large Firm.

Summary:
- Editor of legal journal; published author of legal articles.
- Perceptive in determining direction of research, planning trial, and pre-trial strategy in complex commercial litigation.
- Achieve notable results through expertise in brief writing for state and federal court.
- Trial experience in civil and criminal cases.
- Ability to use CaseMap4, TimeMap, NoteMap, and TextMap.

PROFESSIONAL HISTORY:

1994–present   BALLY, KRASNOFF, SIMMONS, and HEERTZ, New York, NY
Senior Associate (1996–present)
Junior Associate (1994–1996)

Litigation
- Conduct depositions and trials in a variety of media and commercial cases.
- Reduce costs by management of department in creditors' rights and bankruptcy cases.
- Participate in the preparation of negotiation positions; reach acceptable agreement considering objectives and regulatory constraints; saved more than $4 million in 2001.
- Achieve favourable resolution of complex, difficult-to-win cases through deployment of group-supported strategies and reconciling of differences.

Media
- Practised in all aspects of media law for large and medium-sized clients.
- Conducted and directed media litigation including print and Internet copyright issues.
- Avoided litigation through creative merging of legal and editorial skills in pre-publishing libel and privacy counselling.
- Negotiated contracts and settlements between entertainers, managers, and venues.

Management
- Negotiate and administer domestic and international contracts; assure compliance with government regulations and export control laws.
- Select, supervise, and control local counsel in out-of-state cases to assure superior results; reduce expenses by meticulous attorney bill review.
- Supervise and mentor junior associates to focus database searches and briefs.

EDUCATION:

1994   LLB, COLUMBIA LAW SCHOOL, NY, NY – Cum Laude; Harlan Stone Scholar; Dean's List

1991   BA, Political Science; COLUMBIA COLLEGE, NY, NY, Dean's List

PUBLICATIONS: *Columbia Journal of Law and Social Problems* – Editor
Kings Crown Essays – Managing Editor

Comments: Carole's history is ideal for a chronological CV. Her second page shows two distinctly different and equally interesting jobs. She headlines 'Previous Career' to include the job description but avoids the actual dates.

Carole Stevenic

885 Sherman Road • Charlotte, NC 12345
555-123-4567 Home • 555-312-4675 Office
stevenic@internetprovider.com

OBJECTIVE: *Executive Vice-president, Marketing*

SUMMARY:

- Created and produced HARTON magazine; specialized publication for the shipping and distribution trade, frequently quoted in the trade press; circulation of 38,000.
- Created a solid brand image by standardizing graphic images and colour on all internal and external printed communications and packaging.
- Produced special events to gain press exposure; increased name recognition in trade.
- Keynote Speaker at the annual conference of Shipping and Distribution Association.
- Developed and managed Office of Immigration Affairs for the Hart-Compton Group.
- Established reputation as expert in matters of immigration law and procedure.

PROFESSIONAL HISTORY:

1991–present   HART-COMPTON, Inc., Charlotte, NC

Public Relations Director/Editor, Harton Magazine (1996–present)

- Create and produce corporate magazine for worldwide distribution in house and to members of affiliated trade associations.
- Determine editorial policy and objectives with senior management; report directly to Chairman and Chief Executive Officer.
- Review all articles to assure content accuracy and alignment with established goals.
- Directed major reformatting that increased by 20 per cent the number of times magazine was quoted in other publications and broadcast news reports.
- Establish brand image by administering corporate graphic standards, defining the visual style for all company communications to strengthen public recognition.
  - Received Public Relations Society award for branding success by documenting a 15 per cent increase in corporate recognition by an independent survey.
  - Produce ads, promotional materials and web page compatible with brand image.
  - Place corporate logo on all corporate vehicles, packing materials, and uniforms.
  - Direct the activities of writers, photographers, web page, and graphic designers to assure agreed-upon objectives are met.
  - Instituted corporate sponsorship of three major charitable events and secured brand placing in two motion pictures resulting in publicity equivalent to $400,000 in advertising fees.
- Write and publish the *President's Update*, a biweekly newsletter to all employees.
- Write, proofread, and copy edit presentations made by senior management to press.
- Represent corporation to legislators and special interest groups.
- Oversee negotiation with printers on methods to produce quality within budget guidelines.

Manager, US Immigration (1991–1996)

- Managed a complete immigration service for international employees relocating to/from USA.
- Developed, published, and implemented company policy on immigration issues; kept current with issues and revised policy as prevailing laws and regulations changed.
- Maintained full compliance with all laws and regulations.
- Recommended to top management appropriate options for recruitment and relocation of personnel depending upon visa status.
- Maintained liaison relationship with government and legal authorities; coordinated with in-house and outside counsel.
- Prepared petitions, applications, and motions to the Departments of Justice, State, and Labor; saved company up to $150,000 in legal fees.

Previous Career   US House of Representatives, Washington, DC
                   Legislative Assistant

- Researched legislation and background material, working with committee staff in preparation for hearings.
- Designed, wrote, and circulated congressman's quarterly newsletter to constituents.
- Prepared correspondence for signature, proofreading for content accuracy and grammatical correctness.
- Conducted case work on legislative matters through various agencies.

EDUCATION/AFFILIATIONS:

Management Training Programme, Hart-Compton, Inc.

Master's in Business Administration, Marketing
BA – English/Psychology – Phi Beta Kappa
University of North Carolina, Raleigh, NC

Public Relations Society of America, Member since 1991

Comments: Sulani's career is full of clear-cut accomplishments that are better explained in detail in an interview than delineated on a paper CV. He could send a second page if requested. Notice that his objective is perfectly keyworded for scanability.

SULANI D. MURALSIKH

334 Avenue of the East, Penthouse A
Weehawken, NJ 12345
Home (555) 123-4567; Office (555) 321-7654, ext. 59
muralsikh@internetprovider.net

OBJECTIVE

International Economic Development Arena to Apply Expertise in the Following:

Proposal Development International Banking　　**Resource Allocation**　　**Strategic Planning**

PROFESSIONAL EXPERIENCE

1997–present **FEDERAL RESERVE BANK OF NEW YORK**, New York, NY
　　　　　　OPERATIONS ANALYST

Organize and manage the development of operational review proposals submitting documented results to top management with recommendations for action.

Accomplishments include:

- Initiated, systematized, and managed a review of bank examinations and bank applications processing activities, resulting in annual savings of $12.5 million.
- Developed long-range plans, necessary capital, and operating budgets for the 185-person International Services Department.
- Analysed costs of foreign exchange and investment transactions; developed procedures that reduced annual costs by 15 per cent.
- Oversaw the development of a computerized forecasting model to maximize revenue.
- Coordinated bank's efforts with initiatives in the Federal Reserve System.

1990–1997　　**UNITED NATIONS DEVELOPMENT PROGRAMME**, New York, NY
　　　　　　PLANNING OFFICER

Oversaw programme planning, resource allocation, and evaluation of a $100 million programme of technical and capital assistance to developing countries in the area of population control and economic development.

Accomplishments include:

- Organized and supervised a 10-month, fifteen-person study of the world contraceptive market, sponsored jointly by UNDF and the Ford Foundation; wrote initial proposal to secure matching funds.
- Developed a model-based forecasting system for programme planning, management, and control resulting in improved programme response time with 20 per cent cost reduction.
- Developed population-control projects for countries in East Africa and the Middle East.

EDUCATION

1994　　　　PhD International Banking, New York University, Graduate School of Business

1990　　　　MS Management, Massachusetts Institute of Technology

Comments: Alex uses the chronological format since his entire career is with one company and shows steady growth. He has no college credits, so he's left off 'high school graduate', which is assumed.

ALEX IVAN BALLISTER
1438 Linden Street
Allentown, PA 12345
555-123-4567
ballister@internetprovider.net

OBJECTIVE: INDUSTRIAL ENGINEER

SUMMARY:
- Hands-on team leader known for achieving high quality and productivity.
- Ability to plan and improve manufacturing processes through workforce utilization strategies.
- Create cost-containment strategies; implement significant cost savings.
- Participated in evaluation of proposed equipment purchases leading to cost-saving efficiencies.

EXPERIENCE:

1999–present   **BLACK & DECKER** (acquired by GE in 1999), Allentown, PA
Senior Manufacturing Planner
- Establish work methods and measurements; maintain procedure database used in ISO 9000 standards approval process.
- Procured manufacturing equipment; visited vendor sites to evaluate machine tools to produce products safely and efficiently.
- Collaborated in determining realistic but challenging operation goals; team cited by senior management for achieving highest productivity for three consecutive years.

1990–1999   **GENERAL ELECTRIC COMPANY**, Allentown, PA
Housewares Manufacturing Department

Senior Manufacturing Planner (1996–1999)
- Planned and established approved revisions in operations and equipment
  - reorganized work space including all facilities required for tool storage
  - arranged for staff training on new equipment and procedures
  - accommodated production schedule changes with new product mix or design changes.
- Analysed methods, facilities, and processes; made recommendations leading to lower manufacturing costs.
- Recognized for 30 per cent cost savings in first year.

Manufacturing Engineer (1992–1996)
- Evaluated specifications regarding design and materials used in final products; analysed prototype models of housewares products.
- Investigated customer complaints and recommended corrective action leading to design changes.
- Determined manufacturing specifications and cost projections.

Lab Technician (1988–1992)
- Analysed malfunctions in customer-returned appliances; made suggestions for design changes.

EDUCATION: General Electric Technical Training Programme, Allentown, PA.

Comments: Ralph has only a high school diploma, so he leaves off education as a category. He has an excellent career history, so this will not hold him back from getting interviews.

RALPH J. MICHALSKI
344 RADCLIFFE ROAD
BRIDGEPORT, CT 12345
(555) 123-4567 PHONE; (555) 123-4765 FAX
michalski@internetprovider.net

OBJECTIVE

Executive Position in International Sales to Facilitate Increasing Market Share, Profitability, and Corporate Image

SUMMARY

- Experienced in offshore sales, marketing, and negotiation.
- Understand diverse cultures through extensive travel.
- Multilingual with working knowledge of French, Dutch, and Arabic.
- Skilled in establishing competitive pricing and credit policies.
- Increased revenue consistently while controlling costs.

PROFESSIONAL EXPERIENCE

US ELECTRICAL, Division of HAMMOND ELECTRIC, Bridgeport, CT   1992–present

AREA SALES MANAGER/ADMINISTRATIVE MANAGER   1999–present

- Assist in setting sales forecasts for territory covering the Middle East and Africa.
- Administer salary planning for staff of 25 sales and 14 administrative personnel.
- Implement annual budget of $8 million; keeping all projects at or below cost.
- Handle direct negotiation of contracts and projects with foreign government municipalities in Middle East and Africa; achieve desired outcomes by sensitivity to local cultural values.

INTERNATIONAL MARKETING SERVICES MANAGER   1996–1999

- Reported directly to Vice-president of International Sales.
- Managed 16 regional marketing representatives and customer service personnel; evaluated performance on workload measurement and outcomes.
- Directed and coordinated all administrative functions performed by foreign subsidiaries and offshore sales offices; established procedures and practices considering both corporate needs and local cultural values.
- Administered policies on pricing, credit, financing, and goods distribution to increase revenue while controlling costs.
- Established sales incentive programmes and commission policies; sales increased by 15 per cent per quarter for two consecutive years.
- Assisted Vice-president in expense control and budget development.

PRICE ADMINISTRATOR – INTERNATIONAL PRODUCTS   1992–1996

- Administered pricing policies on orders, contracts, and project bids; met annual gross profit targets each year, exceeding targets for two years.
- Analysed sub-product mix relative to product objectives and effect on profit and loss.
- Conducted pricing studies on competing products to guide corporate pricing policy.

MILITARY SERVICE: General Quartermaster, CT National Guard   1998–present

Comments: Juan selects a CV format to highlight his experience in his field and uses specific examples and concrete results to demonstrate his accomplishments.

JUAN RAMIREZ

199 Barbara Street • Torrance, CA 90503 • (310) 555-3233 • (310) 555-9989 FAX
rami@internetprovider.net

OBJECTIVE: Instructor of Food Service Management to develop food service workers' skills, improve restaurant quality, and increase customer loyalty.

SUMMARY:

- Chef with business, catering, and event management experience.
- Skilled in staff development including kitchen skills, sanitation, customer service, and employee motivation.
- Restored profitability to a small, specialized menu restaurant.
- Supervisory experience with a major hotel chain.

PROFESSIONAL EXPERIENCE:

1999–present   CHIEF CATERER, J and R Catering, Lomita, CA

- Cater events from picnics to formal dinners for up to 3,500; develop and serve specialized menus for event themes.
- Contract catering services for parties; major accounts include Lomita Civic Center and Culver City Masonic Temple.
- Develop new business sales that exceeded $500,000 annually.
- Manage staff of 50; increased staff retention by revising hiring and training procedures; mentor new staff to excel in customer service.
- Order food and supplies keeping quality high while controlling costs.

1995–1999   NIGHT CHEF, Inns Way Management, Inc., Seattle, WA

- Supervised five chefs during night shift for two area Radisson hotels.
- Received a four-star rating by the American Automobile Association and *Seattle Daily's* 'Best Area Restaurant' award by readership vote.
- Hired, trained, and supervised kitchen personnel; monitored and coached staff to increase performance and customer service standards.
- Maintained business records including food purchasing costs and payroll.

1991–1995   PARTNER/OWNER, The Grotto, Seattle, WA

- Restored a failing restaurant to profitability in three years; gross sales exceeded $2 million.
- Developed a menu specializing in Cajun and Creole food.

EDUCATION/AFFILIATION:

1991   AS Applied Science in Culinary Arts
            Portland Community College, Portland, OR

            American Culinary Federation, member since 1991

All Piatkus titles are available from:

Piatkus Books, c/o Bookpost, PO Box 29, Douglas, Isle Of Man, IM99 1BQ

Telephone (+44) 01624 677237
Fax (+44) 01624 670923
Email; bookshop@enterprise.net
Free Postage and Packing in the United Kingdom
Credit Cards accepted. All Cheques payable to Bookpost

Prices and availability subject to change without prior notice. Allow 14 days for delivery.
When placing orders please state if you do not wish to receive any additional information.